LEADING PRIMARY
SCHOOL IMPROVEMENT
what works, and why

This book is dedicated to all those practitioners undertaking part-time study to improve their professional practice.

LEADING PRIMARY SCHOOL IMPROVEMENT
what works, and why

Adrian Smith and Catherine Sykes

Peter Francis Publishers

Peter Francis Publishers
The Old School House
Little Fransham
Dereham
Norfolk NR19 2JP UK

**A CIP catalogue record for this book
is available from the British Library**

ISBN 1-870167-36-8

Printed and bound in Great Britain by Biddles Ltd,
Guildford and King's Lynn.

Contents

Foreword

I AM very pleased to be asked to write a foreword to *Leading Primary School Improvement: what works, and why* for a number of reasons. This volume makes a novel contribution to the debate about educational research. The quality and relevance of much educational research has been questioned by a number of authorities in recent years. It has been dismissed as trivial, as lacking rigour and of failing to inform professional practice. Notwithstanding these criticisms of educational research, teachers have been exhorted to establish themselves as an evidence-based profession in which research plays a major role in informing both practice and decisions about practice. At the same time, educational researchers have been encouraged both to value and to celebrate research conducted by practitioners, by head-teachers and teachers in schools.

This book is partly recognition of the value of practitioner research. It illustrates how complex issues related to school improvement can be illuminated by research conducted in schools. Within these pages is also contained a celebration of that significant research tradition. Each of the chapters demonstrates how dedicated tutors have introduced the teacher researchers to the techniques of research and encouraged them to conduct their own research projects. The outcomes confirm that such research is both valid and worthy of publication. This book also provides evidence that staff in schools can and do use research as part of the battery of techniques that inform and support their professional judgements. Some of the issues addressed are familiar, leadership styles, the role of the deputy headteacher and the nature of professionalism, while others represent a newer education-al agenda that focuses on strategic planning, ICT and coping with special measures.

Each of the projects written up here is located within a particular educational context. Each is the product of research and reflection that began as a response to a set of circumstances that existed at a specific time in one or more primary schools or local education authorities. As such, when they are taken together, the chapters of this book provide a collage made up of the concerns and enthusiasms of staff in primary schools. It shows a willingness to wrestle with the problems of innovation in a variety of fields and an admirable capacity to respond positively to the most challenging of circumstances. It is, therefore, a testament to the capability and resilience of the practitioner researchers who conducted these projects and those with whom they work.

More importantly, however, *Leading Primary School Improvement: what works, and why* is a celebration of both personal and professional growth. For a number of years I had the privilege to be the external examiner for the academic programme that has underpinned the research projects reported here. I witnessed at first hand the struggles and the successes of both students and tutors as, together, they sought to explore the inner world of educational research and to make it professionally relevant. The tutors had to help their students to acquire the necessary skills and techniques while, at the same time, not allowing them to become overawed with the tasks that faced them. The practitioner researchers, working largely in the twilight zone, had to cope both with the demands of challenging full-time posts and the rigour of part-time study for a higher degree. Their success is recorded in these pages.

Les Bell, Professor of Educational Management
Management Development Unit
School of Education
University of Leicester

Acknowledgements

We are indebted to Katherine Straker, Research Co-ordinator at Edge Hill, for all her editorial advice, guidance and practical help with chapters and also the CPD administration staff.

Confidentiality

Much of the material gathered by our researchers was given on the understanding that anonymity would be preserved, hence all names have been changed and descriptions left deliberately vague to preserve the confidentiality of respondents.

Adrian Smith and Catherine Sykes

Chapter One

Introduction

THAT the teacher associations were to increase their participation in educational research is to be applauded, not just for reinforcing their credibility further as a respected voice in the professional dialogue but also as another valuable access route for teachers keen to make their research findings public. Similarly, Michael Barber's article (2000a) outlining the website discussions hosted by the National College for School Leadership, was a further illustration of the commitment of a profession that already appears to work substantially longer hours than the European Working Time Directive would advocate. Given the passion for their work is it surprising, therefore, that such highly contentious (and organisational unproven) issues as performance-related pay occasionally spill over into the realm of posturing during the traditional Easter conference season? We must not forget, however, that by any yardstick schools have become more effective over the last decade and, as Drucker (1979) reminded us:

> the difference between an effective organisation and an ineffective one is the performance of the people. No amount of tabloid criticism or official sniping can contradict this.

However, when it comes to measuring the dimensions of such improvement, the waters are rapidly clouded by outsiders who are intent on constructing batteries of checklists as a means of jump-starting one failing school from the leads of another. It is in this area that teachers need a stronger voice, and politicians should tread lightly whilst school improvement researchers and consultants, not directly working in classrooms, are perhaps better qualified to coach from the touchline rather than play the position of leading striker. In a recent lecture on influencing policy through qualitative research, Professor Gareth Williams (2000) referred to the means of providing answers to questions from a contextual viewpoint, identifying the form and nature of what exists. We would argue that nobody is in a better position than the teacher researcher to demonstrate this strand of re-search evidence. We have resisted calling in the favours of former colleagues and visiting the prime sites (along well trodden paths), imposing ourselves on busy staffrooms or interviewing anxious teachers only to leave with a superficial awareness or suspicions of window dressing undertaken to impress higher education guests. Instead, we have drawn on the resources of people who have worked with us on continuing professional develop-ment (CPD) courses, through their postgraduate certificates, diplomas and finally awarded MAs on the basis of their final dissertations. Not just head-teachers (although their perspectives have proved invaluable), but deputies and senior staff, all of whom enjoy the credibility and goodwill of colleagues and as a result can gain easy access and hence be more selective in the estab-lishment of a balanced sample that will hopefully reflect the diversity of opinion.

Many of the subjects are not new: a snapshot of professionalism, marketing, the role of the deputy headteacher, leadership styles are all familiar territory. However, other areas concerned with strategic planning, innovation, managing information communication technology (ICT) and approaches to the failure of schools in special measures perhaps provide a fresh dimension to the improvement debate. Whilst the chapters offer no ex-plicit answers there are a number of recommendations and discussion points that can only broaden the debate and help shape the focus of why and what works in the modern primary school. Qualitative research plays an impor-tant role alongside the statistics and performance league tables, but the integral role of hands-on professionals should never be overlooked.

It is for this reason that the announcement of best practice scholarships, honouring a pledge made in the White Paper (1997), was welcomed. Whilst there has been no intention to review in this book Labour's policy record in education, nevertheless their return to office mirrored the three year time-span taken by many of our researchers to complete their studies. Hence, in 1997, as the then Leader of the Opposition, Tony Blair, was reminding the electorate of his 'three' education priorities, behind the scenes other members of the 'B' brigade, Professor Michael Barber and the then Shadow Secretary of State David Blunkett and future Schools Minister Steven Byers, were identifying key areas of policy to outline to Parliament some ten weeks later. As *The Times* reported on June 23rd that year, 'the pace of change since May 2nd has left civil servants gasping'. Under the headline "Dramatic transformation to a great ministry", the article went on to preview the education and employment team, beginning with the Secretary of State who was then still 'enjoying a honeymoon period with teachers and parents, although some colleagues resent his conversion to Blairite policies'.

At that time, according to *The Times*, the in-tray for education included developing a 'more positive' inspection system, decisions about eighteen failing schools, speeding up the dismissal of incompetent teachers and meeting the highly ambitious targets for primary schools. Restoring morale in the teaching profession with talks on the establishment of a general teaching council formed the basis of proposals on the management agenda whilst, in addition, administrative decisions on school repairs, class sizes and nursery provision needed to be faced.

Against this background, the White Paper could justifiably be termed a new approach or, as *The Times Educational Supplement* (1997) noted in its leader of that week, "Passion in Action", 'it has been a good week for David Blunkett and his White Paper which has appeared to almost universal acclaim'. The article went on to commend 'the jigsaw of interlocking policies which offer a coherent and comprehensive programme'. Later in the balanced critique there was concern regarding the translation of aspiration into meaningful action:

> How can enormous amounts of effective in-service training – and the cover for which such a programme requires – be achieved on a shoe string? Can local authorities be expected to play a stronger role in monitoring schools, if at the same time they have to delegate yet more money?

Many of these issues have been addressed by our researchers to some extent, ensuring that chapters provided a topical focus coupled with an authoritative commentary on events as seen from the classroom rather than the council chamber. Part of the White Paper, on standards and accountability, provided the springboard for many researchers to gauge the impact at school or classroom level. Perhaps the most wide-ranging research was that of Boyes with his questions of leadership, professionalism, continuing professional development, and school improvement which, with opinions gathered from the more extended professionals, passed judgement on a raft of proposals in a balanced critique including comments on performance pay, inspection and standards.

More specifically, Chapter 6, on improving development planning in primary schools, is a good illustration of White Paper ideals being translated into practical approaches. What emerged, however, was still a lack of clarity by many education professionals, together with an unwillingness by many governors to be involved. The exception in the researcher's case study confirmed the benefits of including business analysts, particularly in the realm of target setting and maximising performance data.

A similar theme ran through Bennett's survey in Chapter 3 on innovation and change where the DfEE, DTI (1997) framework was adapted to research innovation strategies by headteachers. As has been recorded in the chapter, given the enormous changes that have taken place in primary schools since 1995, together with their impressive gains in pupil performance, there would now appear to be much that other organisations in the commercial and industrial field could learn from the successes of school leaders in change management.

The White Paper also focused on action to tackle under-performance and specifically the role of Office for Standards in Education (OFSTED). Merry's research, recounted in Chapter 9, carried out with schools in special measures, focused on many of these points with examples of how the system was slow to react particularly regarding the role of the local education authority in providing early warnings. The statement in the White Paper 'where an LEA has concerns it should intervene in a number of ways' was found to be largely aspirational rather than practically focused, particularly in many cases where the advisory support was often rotated and despite many staff being aware of deep-seated problems there appeared no outlet through which to voice their concerns.

At the same time however other teachers are without doubt making great strides in their professional practice. School leadership and professional development for the deputy headteacher reflect two other themes. Goggin, as a researcher, represented many across the county as an experienced deputy headteacher undertaking a demanding management role. What emerged from her study was a general acceptance of change within a supportive environment although the concerns of having too many initiatives prescribed from the centre were never far away.

There was also a focus in the White Paper on school leadership, an area that a newly appointed headteacher researched with interesting results. Issues of skills and competencies for a mandatory headship qualification and the question of a fast track route remained at the forefront of government thinking. Yet as Parkinson commented: 'Three very different pictures emerged. It is perhaps in these areas (vision, strategic management, communication) that the uncertainties surrounding the first year of a new headteacher have been most obvious.'

While the White Paper included sections on accelerated learning, specialist schools and action zones, by far the most wide reaching, however, were the paragraphs on a National Grid for Learning (NGfL), containing a ten-year strategic commitment to unlock the potential of ICT in every school in the country. Drawing on evidence from the DfEE (1998) survey that identified the need to support and train teachers as well as increasing their confidence, the government pledged National Lottery funding and a public private partnership to deliver services to learners across the board. Singleton's research (see Chapter 4) concentrated on these developments at the grass roots in schools in a large shire county local education authority. As an advisory teacher for ICT she was well placed to evaluate what had been achieved so far, as well as making recommendations for the future. Despite a number of positive findings, there remained clear evidence (gathered from an enlightened sample) of multiple responsibilities and insufficient resources for co-ordinators to achieve the kind of impact enjoyed by recent literacy and numeracy initiatives. Yet, whilst co-ordinators remained optimistic about the future potential of technology in both administrative and curricular terms, the practicalities and, particularly, the role of the local education authority as a catalyst, cast a shadow over any rapid development.

Finally, it is worth remembering that school improvement takes many forms, not the least in image promotion and alignment of the many stakeholders and clients. For this reason Core's research on marketing (see Chapter 8) within the primary school contained messages regarding ethos, leadership and accountability to the local community. The White Paper referred to fairer funding for all categories of schools as well as outlining proposals to examine local arrangements for the organisation of school places. Parental preference and the criteria for deciding applications were related issues in a study of marketing strategies. As Core stated: 'the process of marketing and promoting a positive image sharpens the process of self-evaluation which consequently strengthens the school.'

In matching these studies to the government's commitment to education it is by no means intended to restrict their sources or inspiration. Their relevance is drawn from researching practitioners, all of whom are well equipped to comment and provide detailed feedback on initiatives. *The*

Times Educational Supplement (1998) reported a little over a year after the publication of the White Paper

> In the 13 months since Labour took office the Department for Education and Employment has undergone major changes due mainly to the introduction of non-civil servant political advisers. With seemingly one division having increased three-fold to more than 100 people the intention to develop new ways of working and directly influence what happens in schools has apparently been bought at a high price.

Most recently the *Times* columnist Simon Jenkins (2000) attacked plans by the Conservative party for all schools to be free of local councils by claiming that the idea of abolishing local education authorities 'was espoused by John Patten, ... developed by Gillian Shephard and is being implemented by David Blunkett in a frenzy of centralist initiatives'. Many commentators would trace the trend back to 1987 and Kenneth Baker's plans to shake up the management of the education service. Writing at the time, Norman Flynn of the London Business School referred to the 'Secretary of State designing a classic machine bureaucracy. Objectives are issued from the top and information about achievements is generated down the organisation and transmitted upwards'. Going on to quote Henry Mintzberg that has echoes for teacher professionalism, Flynn stated 'the more professional an organization the more decentralised its structure', moving on to claim,

> The sources of this decentralization was the power conferred on the professionals by their expertise. The corollary is that centralization denies the expertise of the professionals and reduces their power and status.

Perhaps it is worth remembering that few of those interviewed for these projects were in anything other than the foothills of their career when such reforms were introduced. For them, therefore, accountability and standards measured against budgets and efficiency have become the norm.

Notwithstanding such high expectations, the opportunities for professionals to engage in research in its widest forms have never been greater. The DfEE proposals (2000a) recognised the need to encourage reflection on practice in its widest forms as well as 'raising the quality of development opportunities'. Whilst the ten principles did not specifically include research, reference to a wide range of opportunities and the need to share information widely were hopeful signs of a thaw in the research tundra. Furthermore,

> We want to support teacher research in partnership with higher
> education institutions and other schools. (13)

This, together with the resources created by the proposed professional
bursaries, should ensure that all teachers are given the access to the extended
opportunities they deserve and in almost all cases justify, through scholarship and findings often inaccessible to those outside the classroom. In the
field of education management the National College for School Leadership
will create further opportunities to disseminate good practice. Yet, there
would appear to be evidence of high quality local initiatives contributing to
the pool of research data, as the examples from Cambridge, Exeter and
South East England in the White Paper demonstrate.

Finally, it is worthwhile taking time to assess Labour's vision for the
future based on Professor Michael Barber's keynote speech to United States
of America policy makers in early July 2000. In a section on modernisation
of the teaching profession, the emphasis was on developing and attracting
a new generation of school leaders to perform effectively in an enriched
culture supported by public, private and voluntary sector funding. Barber's
assessment of the problems facing the government included the perception
of central government's top-down conformist stance sitting uneasily with
the slow growth of bottom-up change where a combination was necessary.
If teachers were to be rewarded, then a significant component of their professional contract had to be time to research and disseminate their findings.
As Hargreaves and Evans (1997: 2) reminded us, the more committed
teachers have been 'crippled by conscientiousness', whilst 'policy and
research is continuing to present teachers' work in a negative light'. Few
have no doubt that this only applies to the small minority, but, to para-
phrase Michael Barber, others, including our researchers, working part-time
over three years, have accepted the government's challenge whilst we, as
authors, have hopefully added the necessary support.

References

Barber, M. (2000a) "High expectations and standards for all – no matter
   what", *Times Educational Supplement*. July.

Barber, M. (2000b) "On the brink of a remarkable time", *The Times Educational Supplement*, December.

DfEE (2000) *Professional Development, Support for Teaching and Learning*. London: DfEE Publications.

DfEE (1998) *Survey of Information and Communications Technology (ICT) in Schools*. London: DfEE Publications.

DfEE (1997) *Excellence in Schools*. White Paper. London: DfEE Publications.

Drucker, P. (1979) *Management*. London: Pan Books.

Flynn, N. (1987) "An entry fee that has to be paid", *The Times Educational Supplement*, October.

Hargreaves, A. and Evans, R. (1997) *Beyond Educational Reform*. Buckingham: OU Press.

Jenkins, S. (2000) "The three ratings", *The Times*, April.

TES (1997) "Passion in action" (leading article), *The Times Educational Supplement*, June.

Williams, G. (2000) "Qualitative evidence-based practice". Keynote address, University of Coventry, May.

Chapter Two

School Improvement, Raising Standards – A Snapshot of Teachers' Views

S UCH was the speed and change in education in the last years of the twentieth century that Graham Boyes believed much had been over-looked, with many serious issues being barely considered. Boyes, a primary school headteacher of a north west Church of England school, is well respected in the profession and his diocese, and his sound grasp of education policy and knowledge of developments has always been valued by colleagues, governors and local community representatives.

The Study

Boyes was keen to explore the impact of the changes in education, referring to a 'blur of action often encapsulated into a two-minute broadcast that leaves little room for serious debate or information dispersal'. Using the 1944 Education Act as a starting point, Boyes drew on Russell's (1997) overlapping periods in education to examine the dominant values of the time. Beginning with a thirty-year span, 1945-75, the age of 'profession-alism' that brought together central government, local government and the teaching profession as powerbrokers so that no one group held sway, Russell contended that it was during this period that teachers were accorded their professional status, being viewed as people who could interpret children's needs and provide an appropriate curriculum:

No one group had a monopoly of power and there was a continuing debate about the distribution of resources, and about the organisation and content of education, in order for decisions to be made. In the period of economic growth and prosperity which followed the second world war there were sufficient resources to fund an expansion of education provision, underpinned by a consensus of political commitment to the welfare state. (4)

The next age, 'corporation', 1970-81, was overshadowed by national economic decline resulting in governments exercising a tighter control over education. Russell referred to efficiency and productivity becoming over-riding priorities:

> central government sought to establish its influence over the education system through extending its steering capacity. (5)

Such a capacity was put in doubt when, in 1975, Robin Auld QC, on behalf of the Inner London Education Authority, chaired an inquiry into the breakdown of order and organisation at the William Tyndale Primary School in Islington. Months later, when the Prime Minister James Callaghan spoke at Ruskin College, the demands for information and removal of secrecy were clearly voiced and appeared to spawn the third period, 'consumerism', 1979 to the present. This period coincided with the election of the Conservative party into government, who pledged to provide a value-for-money approach as part of their social market ideology. As Boyes recorded, the three aspects were:

- Centralization – National Curriculum, national assessment, inspection and the ill-fated nursery voucher scheme that created administrative chaos and led to the closure of a large number of pre-school groups
- Devolution – concerned with those areas which in the name of democracy and freedom of choice gave power to a local level (but not local education authorities), e.g. delegated budgets, local management for schools, increased power for governors
- Marketization – an increase in the rights of clients, the parents, to choose schools, a diversity of type, for example grant maintained, city technology colleges and an increase in information from and about schools.

Having identified many of the changes, Boyes considered the nature of professionalism and its links with continuing professional development and leadership, all leading to school improvement. Whilst accepting the broad criteria of specialist services, extensive training, rigorous entry requirements, a commitment to work out of hours and further training, Boyes believed that what was important was the way a profession saw itself being able to serve society and the subsequent expectations by society with regard to effectiveness and improvement. In this sense the national decision-making over literacy, numeracy, testing and inspection eroded the operational power that teachers once enjoyed. As a result there is now little room for professional manoeuvring and judgement. Such a sense of disillusionment is by no means confined to education as other studies have reported (BBC, 1999) with each profession facing greater external scrutiny than was once the case. Boyes believed that OFSTED's presence in schools brought many benefits, despite continuing criticism of their judgements. He quoted Fitz-Gibbon (1999) who argued that not only do fine teachers make poor ideas from government work but that self-regulation is sufficient. For Boyes the weakness with a regulatory body such as a General Teaching Council was its lack of structure: 'There have been disasters in the past when education got it wrong, some were so from the start and some became misused along the way.'

An attempt to remedy such inconsistencies was to instigate a managerial control system for schools, that Simkins (1997) argued would 'subordinate professional autonomy and judgement to broaden corporate purposes'. Evidence of this already exists in performance bonuses, and fast tracking of selected staff whilst limitations on class sizes is a further example of national interference in local organisation. This brings us to the question of future headteachers. Will they be leading professionals identifying professional training opportunities or will career structures be so tightly set within a managerial straitjacket that there will be little scope for individualism or professional expression based on the needs of the school? Already the present system is forcing teachers along a specific path in the quest for more pay. For those at senior management level the necessity to identify particular types of training, required as part of a national professional qualification for headship (NPQH), appears sound in theory but takes little account of the distinctiveness and individual character of each school. Boyes argued that 'as no headship will be the same then no one method of training will suffice'. Here there are echoes of Ribbins (1999) (see Chapter 7).

The Sample

Boyes wanted to canvas the views of a number of practising teachers in a format that would allow him to condense personal opinions without losing the scope for individual responses. Hence the questionnaire, a snapshot that corresponded to a single moment, was felt to be most appropriate. As he recorded it was important to:

- offer the respondent anonymity;
- elicit professional background and information;
- sub-divide questions into groups matching the areas for discussion;
- present most questions as closed but with a scale of response;
- present some open-ended questions in order to elicit more detailed responses.

In discussion, and given the background to the study, it was felt that a random sample of 'extended' professionals about to complete a programme of postgraduate study would encourage more response than by asking a group of headteachers to distribute papers or by using informal networks. Accordingly, thirty-one questionnaires were circulated together with a covering letter from the course tutor and instructions from the researcher. Eighteen replied, illustrating the difficulty of obtaining a high level of re-sponse even from those similarly engaged in small-scale research. Whilst it would have been possible to inflate the sample, either through the columns of the education press or by personal favour, this group best represented teachers, all of whom held middle to senior management positions and clearly benefited from the system. Their experience ranged from four to thirty-one years and the prospects for the majority looked promising with few seeking to exit or transfer out of the system. Hence, whatever evidence of disillusionment or scepticism occurred, it would be likely to be shared by a large number inside the classrooms.

Results and Analysis

As the question of professionalism lies at the heart of this study, the over-whelming agreement found in responses to statement 7 on continuous pro-fessional development (section B) (see Appendix 2.1) is logical. Of the respondents 89 per cent agreed or strongly agreed that by the 'usual definitions', teaching should be regarded as a profession. This left just over 10 per cent who had no particular opinion (figures were rounded up) but in the absence of follow-up questions it was not possible to ascertain why. More interesting perhaps was the fact that only four people listed aspects of their daily work which they considered as not included under the umbrella of professionalism:

- dinner money collection, school visit monies
- backing/mending books
- photocopying
- moving large outdoor equipment
- attending PTA events.

Significantly, three out of the four replies indicated they were working at Key Stage 1 with the other respondent in a primary class. Nevertheless, as Boyes claimed, there was still a need for greater consistency amongst headteachers as to legitimate expectations.

Staying within the boundaries of professionalism, it was interesting that an overwhelming 95 per cent of respondents felt that continuing professional development defined by Boyes as longer-term planned learning which is instigated by the teacher was a right (statement 4). Boyes quoted Craft's (1991) criticisms of the delivery of course-led training that included a lack of relevance and inappropriate site venues. This more than anything highlighted the difference between short-term training needs as information-giving sessions and the carefully planned, rigorously evaluated and monitored developmental courses that were in existence. Furthermore, in a climate of school standards delegated funding it was questionable how long such programmes would continue. Nevertheless, the opportunity for colleagues to exchange views and ideas remains an important motivational tool in the learning process. Garrett and Bowles (1997) referred to the importance of ecological change within the formal and informal organisation of the school, or as Smith (1997) noted: 'It can be argued that a key management task is to shape a CPD culture in school or college in order to promote life-long learning in the profession.'

All of this remains dependent on the influence of leadership, something that Boyes examined in section C of his survey (see Appendix 2.1).

The fact that to some degree every teacher is a leader was never in doubt. However, much more interesting were the 78 per cent of responses that felt the style of leadership at times seemed autocratic. If these people recorded such views one can only imagine how the style was perceived by those less experienced and more vulnerable staff members. A picture emerged with 95 per cent believing that they influenced other colleagues yet no one felt they were allowed to exercise discretion in their teaching role.

Boyes' interpretation was that a clear management structure existed where teachers knew the parameters of their responsibilities. As he said, 'It would require a much larger study to begin to break down this question'. In a commissioned research project for a large local education authority, Smith and Sykes (2000) analysed the effectiveness of curriculum co-ordinators as part of their contribution to school performance and found in all but a handful (20 per cent) that their impact was minimal. Where they were influential in their role of monitoring and supporting staff and leading in-service training, then the impact on the results of the school was considerable. Following on this Boyes considered the leadership role of teachers, citing the national professional qualification for headship documents as evidence of government belief that a degree of readiness for headship can be gained. Here it is worth mentioning the Teacher Training Agency school standards documents on the role of subject leader that identified quite clearly the leadership and team building components necessary for effective performance. In section C of the survey statement 5 hinted at the new accelerated routes into headship for those who could demonstrate competence and achievement gained elsewhere. Here there was no clear objection, merely broad agreement along with an acceptance that the beginnings of an overhaul of the promotion structure had already taken place.

Questions in section D, based on the DfEE (1998) document, were arguably some of the most contentious. They touched on aspects of performance-related pay, that has since led to teacher association dispute and advice over threshold performance, where experienced colleagues are able to benefit financially by submitting evidence of competence, that will promote them above a new pay threshold. Responses here were divided more evenly. However, 72 per cent felt that level of work was a better indicator for rewards (statement 1). As Kelly (1999) pointed out, performance-related pay (PRP) 'encourages individualism rather than collectivity'. Having a threshold for mainscale teachers as a vehicle for school improvement was also generally rejected with no extreme views on either side. Clearly at the time of research there was little attention within the profession and consultations were still taking place. There is no doubt that by now opinions would have hardened as the implications began to appear; nevertheless these views represented a balanced appraisal by experienced professionals.

Section E on school improvement and raising standards comprised the final and most detailed area of questioning and possibly contains the most important responses coming from teachers who will inevitably be the professional torchbearers of the next decade. Here, Boyes asked for comments on four areas, beginning with that of inspection, where, despite not achieving total agreement, nevertheless 82 per cent who had been through an OFSTED inspection felt that the key issues raised were generally known to the school. Boyes' interpretation of this was that schools which have effective internal management systems were already identifying areas of weakness and including them in development planning. Others might argue that it took an inspection to kick-start the process that for some came too late (see Chapter 9). Under 20 per cent of replies suggested that the action plan was not leading to school improvement, a situation confirmed by Fidler (1997) who suggested that twenty years of pressure for school improvement meant that teachers were now much better at identifying weaknesses rather than putting improvements into place. Responses about personal benefits were almost evenly divided, with nearly a half believing there were personal benefits to be gained from the inspection process. Boyes suggested with caution that:

> the results of inspection are given a cautious welcome in helping to provide indicators to improvement, whereas the process before and during, in particular, is fraught with apprehension and difficulties.

Once again it is worthwhile reminding ourselves of the sample. Given their expertise, it is more likely that such a group would feel less threatened and more confident as key staff members.

Standard assessment tests (SATS) and the publication of league tables are now a regular feature of the autumn term's educational press. Therefore, it seemed relevant to seek out opinions on the contribution of testing to raise standards (statement 7). An 83 per cent rejection initially infers that little has changed. However, the responses to the next statement revealed that 89 per cent indicated that standard assessment tests have led to a change of curriculum emphasis at the end of key stages. As Boyes questioned, 'is this a valid way to raise standards and as a result is the overall weighting of the curriculum now properly balanced?' Whilst league tables proved slightly more popular as a spur to raising standards (statement 11), the 22 per cent still represented a significant minority. Boyes asked whether the pressure not to be seen as a failing school was an incentive or whether league tables encouraged a fresh look and some comparison (albeit crude) to be made. Again the background of the sample is a factor with a disproportionately higher number of respondents working in effective schools. Yet, in terms of accuracy, respondents to statement 12 were in no doubt regarding the inability of league tables to provide accurate information. The final question of exactly what was the most important component for raising standards provoked a range of responses.

Reflections on the Study

There is much in this snapshot from which both sides, government and the teaching profession, could take comfort, particularly in some areas, for example, inspection and professional development, where the divide narrowed considerably. One key area of conflict remained, however, that of performance indicators of success. The clear rejection of standard assessment tests, coupled with the change of curriculum emphasis, are a cause for concern. Their value as a tool for school improvement, rather than as a weapon to punish those staff failing to achieve predicted results, still appears a long way off as Ouston (1999) recorded in her BEMAS keynote address: 'Negative judgements are made much more frequently in schools serving disadvantaged families'.

Is it any surprise that a curriculum dominated by core subjects and boosted through targeting those just below the level 4 norm should reign supreme, providing echoes of the beginnings of the twentieth century rather than visions of the start of the twenty-first?

Reforms are no longer the preserve of one political party. As Boyes suggested, those teachers who felt a change in political leadership would halt reforms were never more wrong. Yet this is in no way confined to education, as Charles Leadbetter of the Demos think-tank argued in a recent Radio 4 broadcast. Changes are taking place across the whole of the welfare state in a move from dependency to partnership. For professionals encharged with responsibilities to ensure initiatives work successfully at local level, the feeling of being trapped between the rocks of national initiatives is a common one. At the same time responding to the local pressures of increasingly knowledgeable and assertive parents concerned about general standards and individual progress, has become increasingly difficult. One thing is certain, changes in the landscape are profound and, in that sense, it would be unfair to label professionals as 'obstructionist' particularly when measured against their medical or legal counterparts. Despite the moves towards the re-shaping and provision of financial incentives for new recruits, along with structural programmes for the newly qualified, the bulk of teachers who have successfully shouldered a large number of reforms, coupled with delivering performance levels well above expectations in a climate of contractual uncertainty, still represent a committed silent majority. For them, satisfaction is lodged in the transmission of worthwhile experiences to the best of their ability, given the limited resources available. Further evidence of a commitment to improvement can be found in the collective belief in the value of continuous professional development, where the only reservations lie in the rigidity of formal structures that might detract from classroom teaching. Hence it comes as no surprise that a large majority felt that the level of work was a better indicator for reward, as shown in the outcome of section D, statement 1. What is more important is how the impact of performance-related pay will affect teacher collegiality and the cult of individualism. Yet again it appears that a centralist tendency has overruled the local management philosophy in order to create an unwieldy system that might well inhibit rather than enhance the status of many professionals.

Recommendations

- There should be greater consistency amongst headteachers as to legitimate expectations
- Teachers' responsibilities should be more clearly outlined in model job descriptions as part of threshold reforms
- Publication of standardised assessment tests should be available only to parents and results produced to show three-yearly trends as part of a school self-evaluation triennial review that is submitted as evidence to OFSTED

Appendix 2.1: Survey of Teachers

A. Personal Background

(1) Name _____

(2) Are you male/female?

(3) How many years is it since you qualified as a teacher? _____ years.

(4) Which key stage do you *mainly* work with?

Key Stage   1   2   3   4

OR a combination of _____ and _____

(5) My role title is _____

B. Continuous Professional Development

For this section I have defined 'training' as either very short-term courses (1 day/3 evenings) or required attendance at meetings to introduce LEA and national initiatives. 'Continuous Professional Development' (CPD) is defined as longer term, planned learning which is instigated by the teacher leading to personal growth in teaching.

(1) All teachers should be guided through a CPD programme over their time in the profession.

Strongly agree   1   2   3   4   5   strongly disagree

(2) CPD choices should be wide ranging.

Strongly agree   1   2   3   4   5   strongly disagree

(3) CPD should benefit the school as well as the teacher.

Strongly agree   1   2   3   4   5   strongly disagree

(4) CPD should be recognised as a right and adequately funded.

Strongly agree   1   2   3   4   5   strongly disagree

(5) Teachers should be required to receive appropriate CPD *before* applying for a promotion.

Strongly agree   1   2   3   4   5   strongly disagree

(6) There should be a nationally recognised career structure (with options) for teachers.

Strongly agree   1   2   3   4   5   strongly disagree

(7) By any of the usual definitions teaching should be regarded as a profession.

Strongly agree   1   2   3   4   5   strongly disagree

(8) Pay should be linked to CPD success.

Strongly agree   1   2   3   4   5   strongly disagree

(9) Appraisal targets each year should lead to CPD availability.

Strongly agree   1   2   3   4   5   strongly disagree

C. Leadership

(1) To some degree every teacher is a leader.

Strongly agree   1   2   3   4   5   strongly disagree

(2) The *style* of leadership in this school is.

Autocratic   1   2   3   4   5   collegiate

(3) I influence some/all of my colleagues in the leadership role I have.

Strongly agree   1   2   3   4   5   strongly disagree

(4) In my role I am allowed to exercise.

Total discretion   some   very little   no discretion at all

(5) Headteachers should be drawn from those classroom teachers identified as good classroom practitioners.

Strongly agree   1   2   3   4   5   strongly disagree

D.   The Green Paper

(1) Financial incentives for teachers should be for the *level of work* and not for the *star performer*.

Strongly agree   1   2   3   4   5   strongly disagree

(2) Headteachers are the best placed people to appraise teachers.

Strongly agree   1   2   3   4   5   strongly disagree

(3) Having a threshold for mainscale teachers will lead to better teaching and school improvement.

Strongly agree   1   2   3   4   5   strongly disagree

(4) Standards will rise when proper financial rewards are provided for class teachers.

Strongly agree   1   2   3   4   5   strongly disagree

E.   School Improvement/Raising Standards

(1) In which school term and year did you last have an OFSTED inspection?

Autumn/Spring/Summer 1999.

(2) Were the key issues raised *generally* areas you were aware of?

Yes/No

(3) I feel that the OFSTED inspection and action plan led/is leading to school.

Strongly agree   1   2   3   4   5   strongly disagree

(4) I feel that there were personal benefits from the inspection process.

Strongly agree   1   2   3   4   5   strongly disagree

(5) Governors actions and decisions in this school directly lead to school improvement.

Strongly agree   1   2   3   4   5   strongly disagree

(6) Continuous professional development leads to school improvement.

Strongly agree   1   2   3   4   5   strongly disagree

(7) SATS lead to the raising of standards.

    Strongly agree   1   2   3   4   5   strongly disagree

(8) SATS have led to a change of curriculum emphasis in the end of key stage classes.

    Strongly agree   1   2   3   4   5   strongly disagree

(9) Target setting is a genuine way to raise standards.

    Strongly agree   1   2   3   4   5   strongly disagree

(10) Special needs pupils suffer as a result of target setting.

    Strongly agree   1   2   3   4   5   strongly disagree

(11) Published league tables for SATS results are a spur to better standards.

    Strongly agree   1   2   3   4   5   strongly disagree

(12) League tables give accurate information to parents, the governors and the public about the education provided in the school.

    Strongly agree   1   2   3   4   5   strongly disagree

(13) Please state what in your opinion is *the most important* component for raising standards.

References

BBC Radio 4 (1999) *In Business*. June.

Craft, A. (1991) *Continuing Professional Development – A Practical Guide for Teachers and Schools*. London: Routledge/Open University Press.

DfEE (1998) *Teachers: Meeting the Challenge of Change* (Green Paper). London: DfEE Publications.

Fidler, B. (1997) "The school as a whole school: school improvement and planned change" in B. Fidler, S. Russell and T. Simkins (eds.) *Choices for Self-Managing Schools – Autonomy and Accountability*. London: Paul Chapman.

Fitz-Gibbon, C.T. (1999) "Ofsted is inaccurate and damaging: how did we let it happen?", *Forum*, 41, (1), 14-7.

Garrett, V. and Bowles, C. (1997) "Teaching as a profession: the role of professional development" in H. Tomlinson (ed.) *Managing Continuing Professional Development in Schools*. London: Paul Chapman.

Kelly, A. (1999) "A missed opportunity", *Managing Schools Today*, 8, (7), 23-5.

Ouston, J. (1999) "Education policy and equity in the inner cities". Paper presented at BEMAS Conference, Manchester: UMIST.

Ribbins, P. (1999) "Educational administration and the search for Sophia". Paper presented at BEMAS Conference, Manchester: UMIST.

Russell, S. (1997) "A changing context" in B. Fidler, S. Russell and T. Simkins (eds.) *Choices for Self-Managing Schools – Autonomy and Accountability*. London: Paul Chapman.

Simkins, T. (1997) "Autonomy and accountability" in B. Fidler, S. Russell and T. Simkins (eds.) *Choices for Self-Managing Schools – Autonomy and Accountability*. London: Paul Chapman.

Smith, P. (1997) "Values and ethical issues in the effective management of continuing professional development" in H. Tomlinson (ed.) *Managing Continuing Professional Development in Schools*. London: Paul Chapman.

Smith, A. and Sykes, C. (2000) "The soft fruits of school improvement". Paper presented at BERA Conference, Cardiff: University of Cardiff.

Chapter Three

Innovation and Change: How are Primary Schools Managed in Turbulent Times?

HER initial interest in innovation and the management of change was provoked by the experience Gwyneth Bennett gained as an acting-headteacher and a manager in a primary school.

It became apparent to her that there were two distinct aspects to managing innovation; it is one thing to recognise what to do and another to know how to achieve a particular course of action. Her research project was an opportunity to consider how primary schools manage; and to reflect on this management process.

Bennett observed that the need to change and innovate was brought about by both intrinsic and external factors. The extrinsic factors have in the main been imposed by central government. There have been many changes to the primary school sector and the momentum appears to be increasing at the beginning of a new century. Bennett suggested that, possibly due to the pace of change, weak aspects seemed to be the longer-term strategic planning and the evaluation and review of change projects. Quality time and support for a staff to plan and initiate their own ideas, to develop and reflect was often neglected.

Development of the Study

The DfEE, DTI (1997) framework, see Appendix 3.1, was used as a basis for enquiry and also evaluated as a tool for primary schools to identify opportunities to develop their capacity for effective innovation.

The 'partnerships with people' model was developed following extensive interviews with staff from a wide range of companies and organisations. From the interviews a number of interesting paradoxes emerged.

Successful, well managed companies are:

- demanding yet giving
- structured yet fluid
- disciplined yet creative
- confident yet self-critical
- supportive yet stretching
- accountable yet blame-free

The framework report posed the question: 'could any organisation benefit from following these findings?' and answered that, whatever their diversity, all the organisations surveyed depended for their success on *people* to bring new ideas.

Whether a company employs ten or a thousand employees, it requires the potential of all those people to be unlocked if the organisation is to succeed.

Whilst this might be so, Bennett found that in the primary schools in her sample, where ten was the average number of employees, there were positive and negative consequences in having a small staff in relation to innovation. For many purposes the staff were obliged to work closely together. The quality of the teamwork depended on various factors, which included in one school a split site. However, the major influence was the leadership style of the headteacher. There was limited flexibility in terms of time, and the pool of new ideas was small, with staff having two, or often more, distinct areas of responsibility. One respondent commented on the value of trainee teachers in the school for bringing new approaches.

(1) Is there a 'step by step' school development plan which all members   012345
      of staff fully understand?

(2) Do all staff contribute their ideas about how objectives can be imple-   012345
      mented?

(3) Is the school's development plan widely discussed before it is agreed?   012345

(4) Would all staff say that 'management is fair and that every member   012345
      of staff is respected'?

(5) Do both staff and managers expect that everyone will be dedicated   012345
      and professional?

(6) Does the school culture encourage confidence and a 'can-do'   012345
      attitude?

(7) Is everyone highly skilled to perform their job?   012345

(8) Does everyone feel that they are developing new knowledge and   012345
      skills?

(9) Are people being deliberately developed to their full potential to   012345
      benefit?

(10) Do all members of staff work in effective teams?   012345

(11) Are there arrangements in place to ensure that teams co-operate?   012345

(12) Are staff in teams that form and re-form to solve problems?   012345

(13) Is there frequent and open communication down and across the   012345
      school?

(14) Is there comprehensive and open communication flowing up the   012345
      school so that senior?

(15) Is there good communication and strong links within the com-   012345
      munity?

Ratings: 0 to no extent, 1 to little extent, 2 to a slight extent, 3 to a moderate
extent, 4 to a great extent or 5 to a very great extent

Figure 3.1:   The modified pilot and main study questionnaire

How the Research was Undertaken

Investigation was undertaken in five north west of England primary schools, each with approximately two hundred children on roll. Survey methods of enquiry were deemed most likely to provide useful, manageable data on the climate for innovative practice and the process of change. The questionnaire from the DfEE, DTI (1997) framework (see Appendix 3.2) was adapted and distributed to teachers and non-teaching members of staff in the sample primary schools. Both the interviews and the questionnaires were piloted, in a school similar to those in the main sample, and consequently modified slightly (see Figure 3.1). These questions on the five 'pathways' contained in the framework provided an audit of the schools' cohesion in relation to planning, culture, professional development, teamwork and communication. It also provided a context for the analysis of data from the interviews.

The stages are identified by adding together the scores for each group of questions and assigning them as follows:

Score		Stage
0 – 5	Starting Out	1
6 – 10	Moving Forward	2
11 – 15	New Horizons	3

Headteachers

Schools

Pathways	A	B	C	D	E
Shared Goals	3	3	3	3	3
Shared Culture	3	3	3	3	3
Shared Learning	3	3	2	3	3
Shared Effort	3	3	2	2	2
Shared Information	3	3	2	3	3

Deputy Headteachers   **Schools**

Pathways

	A	B	C	D	E
Shared Goals	3	2	3	2	3
Shared Culture	3	3	3	3	3
Shared Learning	2	3	3	3	3
Shared Effort	3	2	2	2	2
Shared Information	3	2	3	3	3

Curriculum co-ordinators   **Schools**

Pathways

	A	B	C	D	E
Shared Goals	3	2	3	2	3
Shared Culture	3	3	3	3	3
Shared Learning	3	3	3	3	3
Shared Effort	3	3	2	2	3
Shared Information	3	3	3	3	3

Non-teaching staff   **Schools**

Pathways

	A	B	C	D	E
Shared Goals	2	3	1	2	3
Shared Culture	3	3	3	3	3
Shared Learning	2	3	3	3	3
Shared Effort	2	3	2	2	3
Shared Information	3	2	2	3	3

Figure 3.2:   Results of partnerships with people questionnaire

Partnerships with People Questionnaire

No schools scored in the lowest category, 'starting out', in any of the pathways, with the exception of one path indicated by one non-teaching member of staff in School C (see Figure 3.2). This according to the model suggested that schools have already developed a collegial approach that will provide the climate for successful innovation. As Bush (1995) noted:

> Collegial models assume that organisations determine policy and make decisions through a process of discussion leading to consensus. Power is shared among some or all the members of the organisation who are thought to have a mutual understanding about the objectives of the organisation.

It is perhaps unsurprising that experienced teachers speak with familiarity about a collaborative approach within their organisations. Writers on education management (Caldwell and Spinks, 1988; Hargreaves and Hopkins, 1991) have been advocating this style of school management for many years.

Dimmock and O'Donoghue (1997), in a study of innovative principals, identified three common traits:

> First they believe in a 'whole school reform' approach. Second, they understand the importance of establishing the preconditions for change and innovation; an understanding which makes them strong advocates of preparing the ground work, cultivating the culture and building a positive climate for change. Third they approach the management of change and innovation in a noticeably 'structured' way.

This would suggest that successful innovation went beyond a bland acceptance of the language of people-centred management and required a deeper analysis of the organisation.

The 'partnerships with people' model advocated simultaneous and integrated development on all five fronts for optimal conditions. Where the assessment tool showed up areas of weakness they should be addressed first. The areas identified in the model and the practical suggestions for organisations to consider following the audit were based on familiar concepts within management literature. Kotter (1990) indicated that innovation did not have to be new or exclusive to 'magical leaders':

developing good business direction isn't magic. It is a tough, sometimes exhausting process of gathering information. People who articulate such visions are not magicians but broadbased strategic thinkers
who are willing to take risks. Nor do visions and strategies have to be
brilliantly innovative, in fact some of the best are not.

The highest scoring, 'new horizons', was for shared culture, demonstrating an expectation of professionalism and a confidence in the schools'
ability to meet challenges based on respectful management.

The lowest scoring was for shared effort and teamwork. Middle-range
scores, 'moving forward', were given by staff at all levels: headteacher, deputy headteacher, co-ordinator, other teachers and non-teaching staff. The
questions for this category related to the conditions necessary to plan for
and implement whole school innovations. Reynolds (1999) writing about
school and teacher effectiveness identified:

> a 'nodding-dog' syndrome in which everyone writes plans, nods, says
> the plans are going to be implemented and then carries on teaching the
> same way as before.

It is interesting that one recent argument against performance-related
pay has been that it would have a detrimental effect on teamwork and
shared effort, and yet in this small sample it seems that the foundations of
collaborative working may not be as strong as imagined.

Contrasting the high scores for shared culture with relatively lower ones
for shared effort it may be that schools are both confident and supportive
but not yet sufficiently self-critical and stretching.

All headteachers believed goals were shared and development planning
well integrated into working practice. However, significantly, three deputy
headteachers and a number of other staff were less sure about this. This was
the second lowest scoring category. The overall scores painted an optimistic
picture. However where there were doubts about the extent to which the
planning process was embedded into school life, coupled with a lack of
confidence in working together to problem solve, schools might not have
the capacity to sustain a strategic approach to change and innovation.

From the data school E achieved high scores at all staff levels, across the
five pathways. Schools C and D identified clear areas of weakness. There
was agreement at all staff levels about which were the weak pathways in
these schools. This level of consistency strongly suggested that the model

could provide a starting point for school development.

Semi-structured interviews (see Appendix 3.3) were carried out in each of the five schools with the headteacher, and with a curriculum co-ordinator identified by the headteacher as having an innovative approach.

Headteacher and Curriculum Co-ordinator Interviews

The five headteachers, two female and three male aged between forty-five and fifty-five, were found to have had similar routes to headship. They had held a number of promoted posts prior to appointment to their present one, including in two cases secondary experience and, for one, a spell as an advisory teacher for a local education authority. Two headteachers had been promoted rapidly, while others had progressed more slowly. This had implications for the levels of management experience in other roles, such as curriculum co-ordinators, which in turn influenced their decisions and management style. Another factor, which was found to influence leadership behaviour, was the length of time in post. The more recently appointed headteachers tended to direct and those with longer experience were able to delegate and act as facilitators.

There was evidence of leadership behaviour being modelled on a previous headteacher's style. One interviewee, however, had consciously rejected the management style of a predecessor as an example of how not to do it and had developed an alternative.

Managers spoke of 'seizing opportunities', (male respondents) and 'being given opportunities', (female respondent) to innovate; and clearly related these opportunities to their own development. The need to give other staff the same opportunities to develop was stressed.

Each of the headteachers had taken part in in-service training activities and all provided such training for others. Only one of the sample held a management qualification, prior to headship. The others saw their lack of management training as a source of regret, although most had undertaken significant periods of management training since their appointment. One thought that the national professional qualification for headteachers had a useful role in preparing future headteachers.

The co-ordinators in the sample were nominated by their headteachers as having demonstrated an innovative approach to their role or as being open to innovation and change within the school. Their roles were varied. All but one of the interviewees co-ordinated more than one subject area, with two holding deputy headteacher responsibility. In primary schools of moderate size this doubling up of responsibilities blurs any useful distinction between middle and senior management levels and as this study demonstrated enables staff in such settings to work for many purposes as one team:

> Many secondary teachers no doubt would envy their primary school counterparts, one of whom spoke with evident satisfaction as she outlined the practice followed at her school. 'Policy decisions are taken through open discussion. We talk it through at staff meetings. I definitely feel that I have an opportunity to contribute to policy making'.
> (Pocklington, 1993)

This level of involvement in policy-making does not exist in all primary schools simply as a result of a small number of people working together. The commitment to collaborative planning must be contrasted with the results from the framework in all the schools surveyed. The potential for school improvement may rest on a more systematic approach to teamworking than was evident in all the schools.

In a number of cases the co-ordinators' subject responsibilities did not match their degree subjects. Nevertheless, there was evidence that they were providing specialist support. However, overall there was a lack of understanding of the management role of the co-ordinator within schools and amongst the sample. The booklet by the Teacher Training Agency (1998) on national standards set out the core purpose for subject leaders:

> A subject leader plays a key role in supporting and motivating teachers of the subject, and other adults. Subject leaders evaluate the effectiveness of teaching and learning, the subject curriculum and progress towards targets for pupils and staff, to inform future priorities and targets for the subject.

This is a demanding role and one which subject co-ordinators in primary schools are currently unable to fulfil in most cases. From the evidence in the interviews there are barriers in terms of non-contact time for classroom monitoring of teaching and learning. Unlike subject-based training there is a lack of appropriate professional development about the role, and a lack of senior management recognition of what is needed or commitment to involving co-ordinators in the strategic leadership of the school. In primary schools subject co-ordination is different from that in secondary schools where there is a more clearly defined organisational structure. Whilst multiple co-ordination roles may encourage teamwork by reducing the possibility of a bureaucratic hierarchical organisation it also means that co-ordination is undertaken by staff with widely differing classroom and management experience. In addition co-ordination is often not recognised in status or responsibility points. This led one headteacher to comment in the question about delegation 'I know what I should say here, but I am going to be honest'. He delegated on the basis of ability.

Professional development for co-ordinators was not well integrated into development planning. Not all co-ordinators were involved in providing in-service training, but there was evidence of managers planning in-service training together. A mixed and rather limited pattern of activities emerged for co-ordinators:

- dissemination of information about courses;
- management of resources;
- policy development and review.

A consultation document on performance management published by the DfEE (1999) gave guidelines for a proposed appraisal system that came into force from September 2000:

It sets a framework for teachers and their teamleaders to agree and review priorities and objectives within the overall framework of school's development plans.

The document continued: 'Target setting, monitoring and evaluation arrangements are well established in many schools.' The emphasis on teamleaders, a term which was not defined, has implications for subject co-ordination; as does the model of monitoring and evaluation leading to planning within the school development plan. Fidler (1996) regarded strategic planning as:

a deeper, more comprehensive form of development planning ... action planning within development planning can be used to implement aspects of strategy.

To evaluate subject effectiveness and inform policies for the future, that is, to manage strategically, co-ordinators will need to have better planned access to relevant information, including that from the classroom.

Results and Analysis

When asked about constraints and freedoms within their roles (see question 1 in Appendix 3.3), headteachers spoke of having too many roles, attending to other people's priorities and being engaged in activities that did not directly affect the pupils. They referred to lack of time within school that, for example, could be used to allow release time to enable co-ordinators to become more effective. This was echoed in the co-ordinators' responses. Co-ordinators also spoke of difficulties in balancing the roles of class teacher and manager, with one fearing staff rejection. Freedoms were more varied for headteachers, with some referring to sharing values and vision whilst others spoke of having an overview, strategic thinking, planning and evaluation. Co-ordinators spoke of initiating, implementing ideas and supporting colleagues.

What they saw as their vision for future developments (question 2) was not articulated clearly by headteachers. This inability may lie at the root of the disparity between their views about shared goals and those of other staff. The exception was the headteacher who replied that she wanted 'everyone to want to work here and everyone to want to come here'. This was in the school that scored highest in the survey. This headteacher also referred to 'excitement' about the work. Each spoke about specific priorities for their schools, often as a reaction to outside pressure. One commented that head-teachers tended to have a clear vision for a school when they first took up a post but that it became harder for them to renew it. Most of them referred to raising standards of attainment or maintaining them, and the raising of standards of behaviour was also mentioned. External pressures were shaping the vision for the future with some 'waiting' for the new National Curriculum orders.

Headteachers believed that most aspects of school life were open to consultation (question 3) and generally referred to delicate personnel matters as those to be kept from other staff. The 'partnerships with people' audit supports this belief that communication is open. Only four re-spondents placed it in the middle category, and of these, two were non-teaching staff. This may have highlighted an issue about team definition. Headteachers were also concerned with shielding staff from difficult decisions which they felt were their responsibility. Pocklington (1993) found in his research that teachers wanted to be involved in policy-making but did not necessarily want to be consulted on everything. Perhaps it is the difficult decisions that should be debated and less contentious issues decided without protracted consultation.

Priorities, it seemed by responses to question 4 were most often externally determined by OFSTED, and by government initiatives. One headteacher saw this as an irritation that specific school priorities were put on a 'back burner' and that new initiatives were so similar to strategies already developed and implemented independently. In one school the development plan was mentioned as being constantly referred to, with the co-ordinators expected to give regular updates. From the data it appeared that development planning was not spread throughout the staff, with a small number of senior managers setting the priorities. Use of data for establishing priorities, such as performance and assessment and parent surveys, was not embedded in most schools in the sample but was a clear feature in one of them. The role of the governing body was clearly stated in one school. Each school was seen to have quite a different focus for motivation and change. In only two was strategic planning evident in the interviews, across all the questions.

In answer to question 5 about the process of change there was a range of responses, from those which outlined a clear procedure to more vague descriptions. Again answers reflected the need to respond to external initiatives with built-in timescales. One common feature was, however, the extent to which this was understood to be a consultative process, as one headteacher commented, 'a people partnership', with views sought from other staff, parents, governors, stakeholders and so on. Respondents spoke about 'realistic targets', 'performance indicators', 'monitoring and evaluating'. The school development plan was the tool through which the process was managed in at least one school in the sample and one headteacher saw the personal example set as a leader of change to be an important element.

It would have been interesting to have had respondents' reflections in answer to question 7 on the reasons for some initiatives being more successful than others, as they tended to list specific innovations as either successful or unsuccessful without extended comment. In one school worthwhile modifications had been made to planning through staff consultation. In another, staff had adopted collaborative group work to please advisers prior to inspection, with which not all staff had felt comfortable. This seems to highlight tensions surrounding any change programme that has not evolved through an organisation's own, consultative, change process. There was no shared understanding of the purpose and potential of this teaching approach. Another school introduced a discipline policy that proved unsuccessful in practice. Where an organisation has a high level of consensus, the partnership with people framework suggests that it should treat, 'genuine mistakes as a training exercise'. Gaining a Charter Mark had led to improved communication in that school and the process of aiming for compliance with Investors in People was beginning to have an effect on staff development. Perhaps these externally-assessed standards are useful in providing organisations with the 'structure' referred to by Dimmock and O'Donoghue (1997: 146), allowing target-setting and self-evaluation, without the element of compulsion and lack of school autonomy implied by national and local education authority initiatives and resented by at least one headteacher in the sample. They may provide an organisation, perhaps particularly a small organisation, with the framework to demonstrate the features within the paradoxes from the partnerships with people report.

Spending priorities (question 7) were linked to the school development plan. Some teachers were better at accessing external funding than others. Not all co-ordinators held their own budget but there was evidence of involvement in the decision-making process even where they did not. As the school development plans, in most cases, were re-active to OFSTED priorities and national initiatives, so spending was largely driven by these concerns. This coupled with the fact that after staffing had been accounted for there were limited funds available, meant that financial management was not able to contribute greatly to strategic planning. The possible exception was in the school that was having a completely new building.

These findings concurred with those of Giles (1997):

> In about two thirds of the schools surveyed, action plans were not complete enough to control implementation. The school development plan was seen, in effect, as a list of 'jobs to do' rather than an agreed set of medium-term priorities which were being systematically resourced and implemented; monitoring and evaluating progress towards implementing policy priorities was noticeably lacking.

He also pointed out that school development plans provided evidence of centrally imposed reforms:

> The need to respond to central government controls imposed by legislation, statutory orders and 'earmarked' development grants.

Some headteachers felt question 8 about delegation was not really relevant, the size of the school dictating a team approach. Their later comments did not entirely accord with this view, with one headteacher admitting that delegation was a personal challenge and another to delegating on the basis of ability rather than through a more democratic process. Throughout their own careers headteachers had taken opportunities to influence school development for their own learning and need to offer others the chance to take risks (see question 9).

In most cases, however, there was a team approach with co-ordinators having an over-view of their subjects and sharing in in-service training provision. Co-ordinators used a variety of strategies to develop their subjects that included monitoring plans and sampling pupils books (question 10). The level of direct involvement varied from the systematic to the tentative level of offering encouragement and being approachable. There was no evidence of evaluation informing future plans. In spite of the issue of time for classroom monitoring of the co-ordinators' subjects, there is scope to define the co-ordinators' role to enable them to be effective.

Reflections on the Study

Bennett's intention was to discover how primary schools manage change. From the data gleaned from this small sample, she was able to conclude that staff in schools expect to work in a broadly collegial manner. As evidence for this she cited the finding that subject co-ordinators viewed management of their area as a 'freedom'. She believed that the quality of decision-making was enhanced when staff participate and that their involvement was crucial as they carried the responsibility of implementing change.

In a discussion about collegiality she referred to Hargreaves (1994: 195-6) who suggested that official groups advocated a 'contrived' collegiality in order to ensure that national policies were implemented. He claimed that genuine collegiality was spontaneous, voluntary, unpredictable, informal and geared to development. Contrived collegiality, in contrast, was administrative, compulsory, concerned with implementing government or headteacher mandates, fixed in time and place and designed to have predictable outcomes. Bennett did not examine this dichotomy in relation to her findings. Headteachers in the sample were concerned about implementing national initiatives and responding to external requirements to the extent that in most cases they were unable to articulate a vision for their school without reference to such demands. Despite Bennett's strong claims for the existence of effective teamwork, based on evidence from the study it could equally be argued that contrived collegiality is actually in place. A small number of individuals were engaged, relatively harmoniously, in achieving the work of the school whether the work had been defined by senior managers or externally. That there is little time or opportunity for schools to initiate policy limits the potential for team problem-solving. Shared effort (see Figure 3.2) was the lowest scoring category from the partnerships with people questionnaire. Bennett viewed the use of staff meetings to keep developments in focus and maintain momentum as a strength that avoided the possibility of teams expending energy without resultant action. Efficiency and effective time management were clearly important. However, the use of formal meeting dates lent weight to the possibility that hierarchical structures are in operation. The two strongest categories from the partnerships with people questionnaires were shared culture and shared information. The majority of staff in schools appeared to value close working relationships built on trust rather than actively seeking to become involved in strategic management.

Bennett considered that longer-term planning and review of change might be weak in schools. This seems to be borne out in data from the study. Smith and Langston's (1999) model (see Figure 3.3), which was

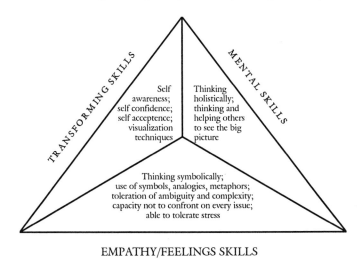

EMPATHY/FEELINGS SKILLS

Figure 3.3:   Empathy/feelings skills, Smith and Langston, 1999: 73 (adapted from Leigh, 1994)

based on Leigh (1994), highlighted three clusters of skills needed by managers of change. Senior and middle managers in schools have many of the 'empathy/feeling skills' that support the other clusters. 'Mental skills' require the manager to see and communicate the 'big picture'. The lack of autonomy in strategic planning at all levels in schools may be one inhibitor of this. Thus Bennett called for 'action learning' to develop team working. This would increase the involvement of staff in problem-solving. It is acknowledged that this would take time but this approach would be powerful in helping schools to become more self-evaluative, collecting both qualitative and quantitative data to inform decision-making. The DfEE, DTI framework provides a tool to aid the process of change management, an action learning framework which could guide decision-making about the goals of the school and how best to achieve them. Without this deep understanding of the school it is difficult for managers to be in a position to demonstrate 'transforming skills' from the third cluster.

Bennett argued for continuing professional development and formal management training throughout teaching careers if all staff were to have the necessary skills to participate in school development planning. Formal management training would only be of value if staff were given, and accepted, real responsibility to manage. The mental, empathic and transforming skills had to be exercised in the school to have an effect on children's learning. The Teacher Training Agency (1998) defined a management role for subject co-ordinators. Teachers would set targets, monitor and evaluate their practice within the new structure proposed for the profession. Use of the national standards and the implementation of performance management may provide the structure for developing a climate supportive of increased involvement, building greater capacity to innovate. At the same time there remain legitimate concerns that performance-related pay may destroy the positive interpersonal relationships which clearly exist in primary schools, as evidenced by Bennett, and which form the foundation for effective teamwork. The effects of yet more externally imposed change have yet to be felt.

From the limited evidence in this research Bennett pointed to the need for a systematic approach to the training of aspiring headteachers. Rather than being reactive, headteachers need to be pro-active to ensure effective schools. The move to make the national professional qualifications for headship mandatory for new headteachers may address this issue.

If schools are to become more confident in managing their own agendas for school improvement they must also become better at self-evaluation. The model provided by the DfEE and DTI is based on ideas of total quality management (TQM). There is an emphasis on continuous improvement. An organisation that uses the questionnaire as an audit tool cannot relax even if it scores highly on some of the paths. Guidance booklets highlighting what to do next and what to avoid at all levels are provided. The framework elicited useful data about schools in relation to this study; that is, it could be used effectively by schools but its effect would depend on action taken to address areas for development. Bennett saw it as a valid and useful approach. From the evidence the strongest elements of primary schools' people power were shared culture, shared learning and shared information. Bennett believed that the reason for these strengths lay in the size of the organisation.

Various questions for further discussion have arisen from this study:

- What adjustments to practice will primary schools need to make to accommodate innovation and change more effectively?
- What could larger organisations, including those involved in industry and commerce, learn from the experience of primary schools in relation to the management of change?
- What are the most effective methods or tools for school self-evaluation?
- What are the implications for primary school management in the paradoxes, quoted from DfEE and DTI framework, at the beginning of this chapter?

Recommendations

- Headteacher training to have a focus on empowerment of staff and transformative skills
- Continuous professional development for teachers that incorporates building an understanding of shared management responsibilities
- A more systematic and clearly focused approach to teamworking
- Review of the expectations relating to the role of subject co-ordinator
- Improved strategic planning following school self-evaluation

Appendix 3.1: The Partnership with People Framework

	Stage 1 Starting Out	Stage 2 Moving Forward	Stage 3 New Horizons
Shared goals Understanding the business we are in	Plan developed from the MD's vision The plan explained to all staff Performance against plan is shared	The vision developed by top team The vision shared with all the people Jobs related to longer term goals	Participative planning enabled Unit planning facilitated Agile planning operated
Shared culture Agreed values that bind us together	Managers are fair and involved Commitment to your customers Start to tackle the fear of change	Build collective confidence Demonstrate you value everyone Face problems be tough	Lessons are learned blame is removed Shape a competitive culture Change is embraced
Shared learning Continuously improving ourselves	Performance measures are defined Employees are trained for job competence Recruit and select with care	People enrolled in their own development Managers are developed to achieve stretching targets High performance is expected	Develop the person Train managers as coaches Build tomorrow's capability
Shared effort One business driven by flexible teams	Managers developed as team leaders Team performance measured Team problem solving encouraged	Teams trained as effective working units Discretion given to teams Teams made internal customers	Inter-team working required *Ad hoc* teams used Build the firm as 'the team'
Shared information Effective communication throughout the enterprise	Communication effectiveness is checked Process for reporting decisions is used Communicate through behaviour	Be open, good and bad news is relayed Process in place to allow ideas to be taken into account Information is shared between teams	Information is available to allow decisions to be delegated Everyone is responsible for seeking and passing information

Appendix 3.2: The Partnership with People Questionnaire

To what extent ...

Path 1   is there a step by step plan to develop the business which all
employees fully understand?   0 1 2 3 4 5
do all staff contribute creative ideas about how objectives can be
implemented?   0 1 2 3 4 5
is the firm's strategy and business plan widely discussed before it is
agreed?   0 1 2 3 4 5

Path 1 Total Score

Path 2   would all employees say 'management is fair and respect every
employee'?   0 1 2 3 4 5
do both staff and managers expect that every employee will be
dedicated and professional?   0 1 2 3 4 5
does the culture of the firm develop widespread confidence and a
'can do' attitude?   0 1 2 3 4 5

Path 2 Total Score

Path 3   is everyone highly skilled to perform their tasks?   0 1 2 3 4 5
does everyone feel they are developing new knowledge and skills?   0 1 2 3 4 5
are people being deliberately developed to provide a competitive
advantage for the firm?   0 1 2 3 4 5

Path 3 Total Score

Path 4   do staff at every level work in high performing teams?   0 1 2 3 4 5
are there efficient mechanisms to ensure teams co-operate?   0 1 2 3 4 5
do teams form and reform to solve problems quickly and efficiently?   0 1 2 3 4 5

Path 4 Total Score

Path 5   is there a frequent and open cascade of communication down the
organisation?   0 1 2 3 4 5
is there frequent and open communication across the organisation?   0 1 2 3 4 5
is there comprehensive and open communication flowing up the
organisation so that top management really know what's going on?   0 1 2 3 4 5

Path 5 Total Score

(DfEE, DTI, 1997)

Appendix 3.3

Interview questions for the headteacher

Background

- What professional development opportunities have you had in your career?

- What contribution do you make to INSET?

- What are your priorities in a typical week?

- Could you outline your career path to headship?

Main questions

(1) What do you feel are the particular constraints and freedoms within your role as headteacher?

(2) What is your vision for the future development of the school?

(3) Have there been, or are there, any areas of school life or work which you regard as not open for staff consultation?

(4) How is it decided which areas of school life or work will be the subject of innovation?

(5) What stages do you go through in introducing an innovation?

(6) In your view, which innovations over the last few years have been successful and which have been less successful?

(7) On what criteria do you base your spending priority for the future?

(8) On what basis do you delegate tasks to teams of staff in the school?

(9) What strategies do you use to provide professional development for your staff?

(10) How do you monitor and evaluate the work of your staff and support them?

Interview questions for the co-ordinator

Background

- What professional development opportunities have you had in your career?

- What contribution do you make to INSET?

- What are your priorities in a typical week?

- Could you outline your career path?

Main questions

(1) What do you feel are the particular constraints and freedoms within your role as co-ordinator?

(2) What is your vision for the future developments in your subject?

(3) How do you influence and involve staff in your subject/s?

(4) How is it decided which areas of school life or work will be the subject of innovation?

(5) What stages do you go through in introducing an innovation?

(6) In your view, which innovations over the last few years have been successful and which have been less successful?

(7) On what criteria do you base your spending priority for the future?

(8) How do you make yourself aware of the work of other staff and support them?

(9) What strategies do you use to provide professional development for staff in your subject/s?

(10) How do you monitor and evaluate innovations in your subject/s?

References

Bush, T. (1995) *Theories of Educational Management* (2nd edn). London: Paul Chapman.

Caldwell, B. and Spinks, J. (1988) *The Self-Managing School*. London: Falmer Press.

DfEE (1999) *Performance Management Framework for Teachers*. London: DfEE Publications. http://www.dfee.gov.uk/excell/teachers/exsum.htm, 30 November.

DfEE, DTI (1997) *Competitiveness through Partnerships with People*. London: Department of Trade and Industry's Innovation Unit.

Dimmock, C. and O' Donoghue, T.A. (1997) *Innovative School Principals and Restructuring: Life History Portraits of Successful Managers of Change*. London: Routledge.

Fidler, B. (1996) "School development planning and strategic planning for school improvement" in P. Earley, B. Fidler and J. Ouston (eds.) *Improvement Through Inspections? Complementary Approaches to School Development*. London: David Fulton.

Giles, C. (1997) *School Development Planning: A Practical Guide to the Strategic Management Process*. Plymouth: Northcote House.

Hargreaves, D. (1994) *The Mosaic of Learning: Schools and Teachers for the New Century*. London: Demos.

Hargreaves, D. and Hopkins, D. (1991) *The Empowered School: The Management and Practice of Development Planning*. London: Cassell.

Kotter, J. (1990) "What leaders really do", *Harvard Business Review*, May-June, 103-11.

Leigh (1994) *Effective Change*. London: IPM.

Pocklington, K. (1993) "Model management", *Managing Schools Today*, 3, (2), 20-2.

Reynolds, D. (1999) "Platform: It's the classroom, stupid", *The Times Educational Supplement*, 28 May, 11.

Smith, A. and Langston, A. (1999) *Managing Staff in Early Years Settings*. London: Routledge.

Teacher Training Agency (TTA) (1998) *National Standards for Subject Leaders*. London: TTA.

Wallace, M. (1989) "Towards a collegial approach to curriculum management in primary and middle schools" in M. Preedy (ed.) *Approaches to Curriculum Management*. Milton Keynes: Open University Press.

Chapter Four

Managing the Development
of ICT in the Primary School

THE establishment of information technology as a statutory subject in the 1988 National Curriculum was the watershed for Michelle Singleton's advisory work. Singleton is an advisory teacher for information communication technology (ICT) within a large north-western local education authority. Her senior management experience equipped her to track developments from the introduction of the first computer initiative into primary schools through to the present National Grid for Learning (NGfL) which demands the establishment of an ICT team in every school, not only to support the curriculum but also to help all staff become increasingly information technology (IT) literate. This led to training the teachers to produce simple yet effective programmes for use in classrooms. Once improved equipment became available the focus turned to integrating the subject into all curriculum areas. It was at this point that Singleton's relationship with schools developed, working with teachers in an advisory capacity alongside college ICT staff.

With the government steering the current initiatives it is worthwhile reflecting on the impact future change programmes will have on schools. The introduction of a National Grid for Learning will involve linking all schools to the Internet by 2002 as well as training teachers to use the equipment effectively to deliver the new curriculum.

Hence, the emphasis here is on pedagogy; the use of ICT as an effective and appropriate communication tool for teachers and children. However, such is the momentum of this revolution that one needs to consider the degree to which subject co-ordinators are equipped to plan, lead, advise, implement and evaluate developments on such a scale, not to mention their first call of trouble-shooter in many smaller primary schools.

The Study

Singleton interviewed ten candidates in total, five class teachers and five headteachers, who were all IT co-ordinators. The sample was chosen from two hundred primary schools which were taking part in the current NGfL project. This she believed ensured that all respondents would have a general understanding regarding the new IT developments in schools. Equally, Singleton felt:

> It was also essential that the candidates had the confidence to ask for clarification of questions if they were unsure about the content. This is particularly relevant to work involved with IT as my own experience has shown teachers prefer to 'keep silent' in unfamiliar surroundings for fear of asking the wrong question. They very often assume that everyone else knows much more than they do regarding IT.

Having gained permission to visit the schools and interview teachers, Singleton recorded that the first hurdle was not the interview agenda, but that every respondent assumed that:

> I was going to solve all the problems in the school regarding IT at the interview. An agreement was reached however, that after the interview had taken place I would be available to them for one hour in order to answer any of their current issues regarding IT within their school. This option worked extremely well.

Such tokens of reward can only strengthen the validity of the process by underlining the commitment of the participant.

Results and Analysis of Interview Questions

Can you tell me about your role in school?

This ice-breaker question allowed respondents to set the scene. As can be seen from Figure 4.1 below all the interviewees had more than one responsibility in school and teaching experience that ranged from the newly qualified to key stage leader, deputy or headteacher.

How did you take on the role of IT co-ordinator within the school?

Answers here went some way to explaining the additional duties for all the headteachers; Emma, John, Tom and Allan had assumed the role as no one else was willing to be responsible. Equally the two deputies, Carol and Gwen, had been placed in a similar position upon being appointed. For the remainder there had been a process of application, either internally, or externally in the case of Jane and Louise; but only one teacher, Jill, received a responsibility allowance for her work in the subject. Clearly there are issues here, not just of funding, but also regarding school curricular development. All too often a major initiative is expected to be developed within a portfolio of other key school management responsibilities, a recipe for overload, frustration and lack of confidence, something explored in the following question.

Do you feel equipped with the knowledge and feel confident carrying out this role and leading the subject?

Although this might have been interpreted as something of a leading question, Singleton's earlier work with these schools, along with the offer of help, had created a more favourable climate of honesty and evaluation. Because of the changing area of the curriculum and need for constant updating all interviewees agreed that they were not confident and at best were trying 'to keep one step ahead of their colleagues'. Three had undertaken intensive training courses only three years earlier (see Figure 4.1) but realised the extent to which the systems and software had moved on. Others expressed concern at the inroads made on their personal time, while those in small schools suffered from insufficient funding to support the level of training necessary. As one interviewee commented: 'I felt confident three

Name and status	Type and size of school	Other responsibilities	Recent developments that have promoted ICT	Sources of support	Experience	Future potential of IT INSET
Gwen D/H	Medium sized 300 Urban – average abilities	Key roles KS leader	Training suite net-worked. More staff awareness needed	Technician shared with HS	Just taken on role training in own time at own cost	Note other priorities in SDP
Carol New D/H	Falling rolls	KS leader	New D/H catalyst	Cannot buy in Needs time commitment	Training course 3 yrs ago. More training needed	More investment and sharing of developments needed
Louise NQT	Village school	Art & numeracy next year 1 pt for IT	IT teaching skills timetabled	NQT non-contact time	IT in industry	Inter-school e-mail communication, info. share, more help from LEA
Jane	OFSTED report special measures proposed	Literacy Co-ord. 1 pt for IT	All staff need to be IT literate cross-curricular	No legislation for IT HMI support LEA	Previous school experience, personal updating in own time	
John HT	Small school	Numeracy Co-ordinator	Curriculum changes Staff training needed	2 hrs per week after school training 2 hrs teaching IT	Only one to identify LEA support	Already considerable changes IT main system

Figure 4.1: Research sample

(continued over)

Emma HT	Small school SM OFSTED	Highlight IT LEA support	IT as discrete subject	Occasional HS technician support	Training case 3 yrs ago personal updating	E-mail, school network
Tom HT	Small school 3 staff	All areas of school re: school very small	Staff confident with PCS	Deficient budget handicap	Personal time for updating	When they receive NGfL funding can purchase new systems + so training for staff
Allan HT	Small school	Maths Co-ordinator + other areas of school	OFSTED trigger Gov. initiatives	Recent OFSTED funding for training	Training course (12 months) 3 yrs ago, IT courses	Need to improve LEA information as well
Jill	Small school (Special measures)	Science 1 resp. pt + IT	OFSTED inspection and NGfL funding	Technician shared with HS	More training for IT co-ord. needed	Funding and resources needed for senior staff
Anne	Medium sized 300+ Urban – difficult area low achievers	Literacy Co-ordinator	Non-contact time Future school budget use	Need comparable training as lit. & numeracy	Previous IT co-ordinator at another school IT ability but little curriculum experience of IT	School budget class administration records

Time commitment – all agreed most of it spent solving technical problems.
More structure

Figure 4.1: Research sample

years ago but you have to keep apace with change which is increasingly hard to do, particularly when there is little funding for training.'

Emma, as the headteacher of a small school, claimed she had had no IT training herself for the past five years, a situation she described as embarrassing: 'As a manager, I have been able to facilitate training for my colleagues, half of whom have a PC at home, but I have not been able to take time out for my own training needs.'

Such a state of affairs is by no means uncommon and brings into question the wisdom of the government subsidising teachers' learning through purchasing grants.

How do you think your role as IT co-ordinator will change in the future?

There was agreement here that the role would assume much more responsibility, as new hardware and facilities became available to schools and IT established itself as an integral role within the curriculum. There was also the recognition that all subject leaders would require greater knowledge and understanding of IT in their subject along with the necessity for technical support. Headteacher, John, viewed his role as numeracy co-ordinator as providing the IT curriculum and the training and support for all staff.

Others agreed that with the current scope of developments it was time to review the role to include more than one person. But for Gwen a deputy headteacher's concerns lay in the degree of technical support expected by her colleagues; something that she saw increasing when a proposed suite of networked computers came on stream. Only she and Jill had the services of a technician whom they shared with the local high school; for others, like Tom, such a fault-finding role was time-consuming and not what they wanted. Sadly, the perennial question of reliability of technology in the classroom was something identified by Jane and others as currently holding back developments.

Nevertheless, Emma and Jane had already started to plan IT into their timetable for teaching as a discrete subject. Gwen, however, was concerned that unless teachers were able to see how technology could help them and their children, they were less likely to accept the changes being presented to them. As she said: 'Teachers will need to be much more aware of using ICT to access the information and what there is available to them on the Internet.' For Anne, the issues of classroom management and organising one computer for use amongst thirty-five children remained a continuous problem. This was a view shared by Tom whilst John said that he 'can foresee the time when all children have laptops to use in the classroom and support for SEN. In all core subjects that will be used more and more'.

Such comments accord with many of the theories concerned with managing innovation and coping with resistance to change. Singleton cited Smith and Sykes' model of the innovation pool that attempts to measure the degree of acceptance depending on the organisational forces and a school's cultural positioning (see Figure 4.2).

Singleton saw the destabilising forces as the continuous changes in software, the fact that ICT never stands still and that an advisory teacher like herself could be introducing new ideas almost on a weekly basis. Paradoxically she saw her role as bringing continuity, raising awareness of change and then alerting staff to the 'countdown' time for a switch-over. Such reassurance is clearly needed particularly when schools go on-line. Other destabilising forces identified were the initiatives taking priority over ICT, and demanding a sense of balance both operationally and in future planning strategies. This led to criticisms of some management teams for their shallowness of support for co-ordinators, something that came through strongly in the study. The Smith and Langston (1999) model (see Figure 4.3) provided some further examples of dealing with resistance.

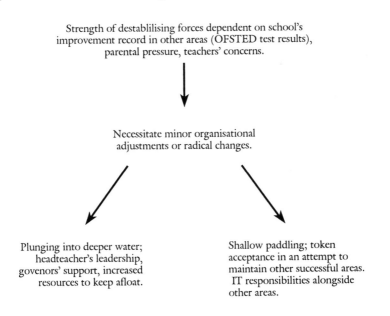

Figure 4.2:   Managing change (Smith and Sykes, 2000)

For over a decade such resistance has been a recurrent theme of business writers on both sides of the Atlantic. Their collective view is that understanding the nature of resistance is the key to the problem; with employees resisting most the social changes that generally accompany the technical ones. Of particular concern is the time available.

How much of your time as ICT co-ordinator is spent in helping colleagues?

Here every respondent agreed it was impossible to put a figure on the number of hours which were spent each week, only that most of it was allocated to solving technical problems. Anne was the only one out of those interviewed who was allocated non-contact time to help with curriculum planning and IT activities for the children. Similarly John was alone in time-tabling two hours a week to allow for staff training and another two hours teaching IT skills to children. However, his reward was already visible in fewer demands on his time as a trouble-shooter. Yet for others the pressure was almost unbearable, Louise as a newly qualified teacher (with no non-contact time) felt that governors and parents were expecting changes to happen overnight. Hence, there was a need to educate them on the need to move forward slowly.

What part will changes in technology play in future administration/ management within the school? How do you think technology will make changes to your role as headteacher?

Anne saw the potential of IT in class administration, reports and records and for headteachers the use of e-mail in a networked community was appealing as it reduced paperwork loads. John admitted that changes had grown out of all expectation in the last eight years, but that all had involved significant time and commitment to maximise the benefits. Improving the information, particularly at the local education authority level, was considered a priority by headteachers whilst in school, Jill felt that senior managers would 'need to allocate serious funding and resources'. Carol echoed this comment: 'We need to develop IT for continuity and progression, we need to share our information throughout the school for everyone to feel ownership of plans and records.'

Examples	Interpretation	Possible solutions
The work of the teachers is undervalued. Unwilling to work alongside 'non-teachers'.	Misunderstandings, selective perception, self-interest.	Finding positive ways of reducing fear – meetings, sharing expertise, resources, views.
Recommendations and/or pledges about resourcing were not kept.	Legacy of previous change and ensuring lack of trust.	Record everything and ensure people are familiar with procedures.
Short-term solutions to satisfy immediate demands.	The quick fix.	Keep staff informed and ask them to look ahead.
Things were better when they knew what was going on.	Security in the past.	Getting them involved in any future plans.
Uncertainties about roles leave them concerned about standards and organisation.	Ill-prepared staff.	Devise shared policies and procedures.
They may be concerned that their own roles will change whether they like it or not – they may worry about becoming slaves to technology or knowing less than the children they teach.	Threats to power of freedom.	INSET focused on the concept of partnership, and class organisation.

Figure 4.3:   Dealing with resistance (Adapted from Smith and Langston, 1999: 80)

What recent developments/initiatives have caused the most changes to occur within your school?

In the research findings this question was linked to the next question in the interview which asked: What took place as a result of this, to the curriculum and to administration and management?

Here national developments, created at the centre as part of government thinking and disseminated locally, dominated the replies, literacy, numeracy, and OFSTED being the most frequently cited. Of the three it was the unfavourable OFSTED inspection report, which according to Jane sent the school into special measures, that had the greatest impact. Not only did this result in a change of headteacher and senior management but the profile of IT was raised in the school. For Emma, the inspection report resulted in a falling of numbers on roll and questions about its viability in the future.

One bonus was substantial funding from the local education authority as part of the NGfL project to help them address the key IT issues. Allan referred to 'prescribed change' claiming 'we are led in terms of change prescription, that doesn't bother me if we are given the tools, plans and resources to use'. In Carol's case, arriving as a new deputy headteacher, the human resource element was the most important as well as raising the morale of staff facing another deficit budget and encouraging them to take control of some of the changes in their curriculum area. Such attitudes to innovation were summed up well by Stewart (1996):

> The training function has a number of contributions to make to the management of change. The first, and perhaps most critical, is to ensure that the 'people' issues and implications of change are raised and understood by organizational decision-makers. Failure to do this is often a reason why planned change does not work out or why organizations respond too late or ineffectively to environmental change.

In this sense the next question on preparation invited answers ranging from a balanced assessment to pre-judged criticism based on ignorance.

What do you feel would have prepared your school for the changes to take place?

Here all the answers reflected some shift in thinking. Respondents were agreed that they could introduce changes to colleagues with greater confidence. Not surprisingly comparisons were made between literacy and numeracy, a five-day block release for co-ordinators in working time. For others a lack of input by the local education authority was noticeable. Emma commented: 'We need awareness-raising meetings which we could all attend free of charge which would lead to adequate training for all. Schools who are in financial trouble are disadvantaged.'

Louise spoke for many when she said it would be beneficial to 'have an adviser to visit the school and to explain to all of the staff the details of the NGfL and what changes would be taking place within County which would affect what was happening within school'.

Clearly, as someone with a background of IT in industry, her comments were founded on observations of successful practices outside education.

Significantly out of the sample only John claimed that support for IT from the local education authority had been good, although once again this was largely due to the recent inspection findings. Carol's pleas for more staff training on a structured basis were echoed by others. She felt that 'people need to slow down and take a team approach to the new changes and not an individual one'.

These last three questions illustrate the dilemma for schools and the local authority being driven by a government impatient for improved results in core subjects yet wanting to be seen as an innovator at the cutting edge of educational technology. Such ambitions inevitably have an impact on quality as Bennett *et al*. (1992) stated:

> Ambitious projects are nearly always politically driven. As a result the time line between the initiation decision and start up is typically too short to attend to matters of quality. The shorter the latter time lines, the more problems there are. The more complex the change the more work there is to do on quality.

But for schools, often the improvements in one area could only be achieved at the expense of narrowing in others. Hence, should they

- embrace the demands for change in ICT knowing that the impact will dampen performance in the core subjects as part of a recognised dip in teacher skill and knowledge?
- seek to embrace change in areas outside core subjects as a piece meal approach to implementation whilst maintaining quality?
- provide lukewarm support for ICT innovation as a delaying tactic, bringing innovation overload in from other key areas?
- delay implementation until resources and initiatives have been fully tested and modified and thus risk condemnation from OFSTED?

Fullan's (1993: 21-2) eight basic lessons are worth repeating here as further explanation of the current deficiencies.

Lesson 1   You Can't Mandate What Matters. (The more complex the change the less you can force it.)

Lesson 2   Change is a Journey not a Blueprint. (Change is non-linear, loaded with uncertainty and excitement and sometimes perverse.)

Lesson 3   Problems are Our Friends. (Problems are inevitable and you can't learn without them.)

Lesson 4   Vision and Strategic Planning Come Later. (Premature visions and planning blind.)

Lesson 5   Individualism and Collectivism Must Have Equal Power. (There are no one-sided solutions to isolation and group-think.)

Lesson 6   Neither Centralization Nor Decentralization Works. (Both top-down and bottom up strategies are necessary.)

Lesson 7   Connection with the Wider Environment is Critical for Success. (The best organizations learn externally as well as internally.)

Lesson 8   Every Person is a Change Agent. (Change is too important to leave to the experts, personal mind set and mastery is the ultimate protection.)

This leads on neatly to the next question which was concerned with school structures.

What do you feel is the role of the senior management team within school in helping to implement any changes regarding ICT?

With one exception the interviewees felt supported by their school management. Most were of the opinion that increasingly ICT was a team approach and like the school development plan as a vehicle for change, there needed to be delegation of responsibilities. For those teachers left on their own there was no doubt that this was a lonely job. Anne felt she was given insufficient help in decision-making whilst Louise, as a new teacher, believed she was often credited with experience in the subject she simply did not have. This need for support and whole school approach was illustrated by Drucker (1993):

Now we are entering the third period of change: the shift from the command-and-control organisation, the organisation of developments and division, to the information-based organisation, the organisation of knowledge specialists. The job of actually building the information-based organisation is still ahead of us – it is the managerial challenge of the future.

Nevertheless such challenges need first and foremost to address aspects of social resistance, those genuine feelings of insecurity reflected in staff comments such as 'I won't be in post if computers can do all the work' or this is the start of a 'technology takeover'.

Here a fuller discussion in relation to schools would have been useful, hence the additional questioning (see Appendix 4.1). Nevertheless, the section on resistance to change is valuable, particularly in the light of government comments linking teacher performance to pay. Lawrence's (1991) views on social change (quoted earlier) opened up another area which needed exploring.

Fullan (1993) took up the same theme, although to what extent ICT changes could be deemed technically simple and socially complex is debatable. Singleton summarised the resistance factors more realistically as

- fear of the unknown;
- lack of information;
- threat to core skills and competence;
- threat to power base;
- fear of failure;
- reluctance to experiment;
- reluctance to let go.

These might well serve as a starting point for an ICT co-ordinators' awareness-raising session on their own.

Setting aside the restraining forces and the use of force-field analysis to which Singleton referred as a possible solution, Bennett *et al*'s (1992) quotation on quality opened up a new area of concern, particularly when considered against a background of the continuous processes that seek to align and re-align an organization to its changing environment. In that sense the dilemma faced by schools is a potent one and it is hardly surprising therefore that despite Leigh's (1994) simplified notions of moving from 'here to there' the complexities of environmental scanning and information-gathering as a precursor to decision-making remain paramount. In quoting Clarke (1994: 137) on crisis change, Singleton went some way to explaining the role of OFSTED as a catalyst:

Without the crisis, indeed possibly even with it, senior management may be very reluctant to go for strategic redirection if it means relinquishing power.

Nevertheless, the empirical-rational approach to introducing and maintaining innovation that sees knowledge as a major ingredient of power translates easily into the realm of the headteacher as co-ordinator, as identified in four of the sample interviewed. For despite attempts at 'building and developing an organizational culture of change' to which Whittaker (1993) referred, for many headteachers the opportunity to lead and control considerable resources remains attractive. Not only does it provide an opportunity to be involved in a high status resource-rich area of the curriculum where many purchasing decisions are involved; but it also means a return to a limited amount of class teaching or group work that can often restore credibility amongst colleagues.

Fullan's (1993) eight basic lessons which arose from the new paradigm of dynamic change referred to earlier might have been examined in relation to the research as a further frame of reference. Instead consideration was given to the role of the local education authority as a supporter of implementation.

For staff in many schools the third period of change as identified by Drucker (1993) is just beginning. Previously IT was largely confined to school administration, with the sharing of machines (often out-dated) between classrooms. Mounted on a trolley the computer could be ferried around to be used for a little word processing that was never likely to impinge greatly on working practices. With responsibility for information technology invariably being given to the last in or new recruit there seemed little to trouble the average class teacher coping with the skills of raising standards of achievement in the core subjects. Now with up to forty hours of training expected to be undertaken in their own time things look a little different, and Smith and Langston's (1999) proposal diagram (Figure 4.4) is of relevance.

In this sense perhaps the following were the most controversial in inviting comments about the local education authority.

Do you feel that there are any other ways in which people/agencies could be helping you to introduce the changes in technology? What should be the role of the local education authority?

Better understanding, more of a strategic overview, improved communication and increased funding, summed up many of the criticisms. Carol made the point that 'schools are not mini-businesses; we have a continued cost implication which we need to address. We want to push forward the

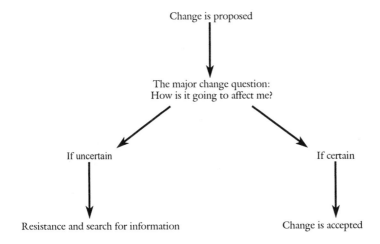

Figure 4.4:   Managing change (Smith and Langston, 1999)

boundaries but need to be confident we can afford to'. This question more than any other illustrated the gulf in knowledge and understanding between teachers and headteachers co-ordinating the subject on the ground and Singleton as an experienced ICT advisory teacher in tune with developments at county level. She recorded the concerns of practitioners about a strategic review before providing a blueprint of the ideal structure in her conclusion. Here it is worthwhile recording Singleton's concluding comments in some detail:

> I would like to begin by looking at changing the structure and management in IT by the LEA. The current management structure of all services within the LEA is well established and included the introduction of the curriculum centre in the early 1980s.
>
> The curriculum centre currently functions under a management structure, which was established originally with the centre. The model is a 'top down' management model and one which appears dated and fails to provide the best and most appropriate service to schools. Most schools were not satisfied with the amount of IT services available to them, however, they were pleased with the level and quality of what they received. It is therefore not simply a question of quality but more a question of quantity. Whilst increasing the amount of staff available

to schools in the form of consultants and advisory teachers, we must also consider whether or not the current organisation and structure of the staff in place is the most effective way of deploying the resources.

Figure 4.5 shows a suggested re-structure of the management of IT of my research findings including curriculum staff, advisory teachers from other curriculum areas and general primary advisers. The role of advisory teacher for IT is now far too big to be considered as 'one role' and we should seriously consider changing the role to that of consultant adviser for IT. The concept of working in schools should continue to take place but with a wider range of people within the advisory division to deliver it. Figure 4.5 suggests the establishment of different groups of services within the IT service.

In the same way in which we consider the role of the IT service and consultants the evidence from the research suggests that we should also consider and re-define the role of the IT co-ordinator.

The evidence from the research sample suggests that this has already begun to take place. The difference in the role within schools is quite marked from one person trying to do everything to others re-cognising the need to establish an IT team in school. It was recognised

Technical Support Team	ICT Consultants	Advisory Teacher Subject Areas and Advisors
1.	1.	English
2.	2.	Maths
3.	3.	Science
4.	4.	Foundation Subjects
	5.	

NGFL Consultants

Lead Offers ICT

Figure 4.5:   Suggested management and support structure for ICT within the LEA

that the future role of the co-ordinator should be to oversee the implementation of the new IT strategies providing help and support for the curriculum as more teachers become IT literate.

Conclusion

The co-ordinators' role has increased with the raising of the profile of information technology within the curriculum. All the candidates agreed that there was a need to recognise these changes and provide national frameworks and guidance for this role. The basic curriculum role should be defined, with extra and additional responsibilities receiving additional responsibility points. We cannot continually rely on the goodwill of teachers giving up personal time to sort out IT problems or finding a friend who can.

Over the next four years, information technology will receive more funding than any other primary school curriculum area. The local education authority and the schools will be responsible for providing the best value and improving standards through the use of this funding. The funding received from the government for the National Grid for Learning has to be 50 per cent matched by the local education authority. Although the process for receiving this funding has to be through the production of a bid by the local education authority, the IT centre can only bid for an amount which the local education authority have agreed to match.

The bidding and matched funding process can seriously restrict the amount of funding available to the schools, a process which should be given careful review at national and government level. It is also important at this point to stress the importance of an effective local education authority policy for achieving successful outcomes for all schools in line with government targets for NGfL funding over the next four years. This should also take account of the amount of staff in place to ensure that all schools receive the most appropriate advice. This may involve centrally funding some consultancy work and courses, which are particularly aimed at providing the initial advice and further monitoring and consultancy work in school.

The NGfL project also cannot continue without future funding and advice. Funding therefore must be allocated into school budgets for the future provision of communications technology. If this is established it must relate to all aspects of the use of information technology which, the research highlights, is a growing concern to teachers and co-ordinators. Support and maintenance of IT equipment in school has nearly always by default been viewed as the responsibility of the IT co-ordinator. This is an area which should be reviewed. There are many aspects of the computer which require management, for example, installation of software and deleting files from the hard disk. Many other areas require technical skills, for example, upgrading the memory, repairing the CD-ROM drive. We must clearly define these areas and provide training for those aspects of this management, which will fall within the role of the co-ordinator.

Training is absolutely essential for teachers if we are to succeed in implementing IT effectively into the primary curriculum. Evidence from the research highlights both training and time to train as essential areas which must be developed in order to achieve successful outcomes. Although this has been acknowledged by the government as a priority with new opportunities fund (NOF) providing four hundred pounds for training for every teacher, it does not provide the basic information technology training which most teachers suggest they need. The local education authorities must provide basic training programmes, which are not in personal time, for all teachers, and the facility to be able to have access to the loan of some IT equipment for a short duration of time.

We cannot assume, as the NOF seems to, that all of our teachers have the basic IT skills, have access to the equipment at home and are prepared to spend at least sixty hours of their own time completing the NOF training scheme. Training has to take priority. The authors would conclude from the research evidence that unless the local education authorities begin to address this at a local level the NGfL and NOF projects will do little to address raising standards in IT across the curriculum.

If we want to address seriously the strategies for change we must provide the means for the implementation of these strategies to take place. The models presented by Smith and Langston (1999) should be considered as guidance in the training process. They provide an excellent starting point for considering the different methods for implementing change. What is lacking is that innovation in this area is not being driven by people who have a firm grasp of how to manage change. Although people may know what they want to achieve, they often lack the understanding of managerial principles which drive the change process.

The provision of IT training is essential, however, so too is the training on strategies for the implementation of change. Initiatives and projects come and go regularly in education and there is no sure way of knowing exactly what will be next and our influence on it. What we are quite certain about, however, is that whatever happens change is certain to follow.

Given its importance, not just locally but nationally, it is perhaps fitting that the Secretary of State for Education and Employment should have the last word. Blunkett in his north of England speech in January 2000 was reminding local education authorities of their responsibilities to challenge, assist, and intervene, all of which apply to ICT if genuine innovation is to occur.

> We cannot be led by the uncertainties, the details of the projects, the people involved. Let us instead be led by the certainty that change will happen and provide the best possible training strategies and support for the effective management and delivery of the process of change within the Primary school curriculum. In this way, whatever initiative takes place we will be ready for and quite certain how to implement changes. This will improve both curriculum provision and access for all pupils, helping to raise standards in the classroom and provide an effective teaching environment for our teachers.

Recommendations

- ICT to be given parity with literacy and numeracy in funding and training grants
- Extend the private partnership with schools to improve facilities
- More support for staff training and IT maintenance by the LEA or through outsourcing
- All schools to submit evidence of their progress in training and resources as part of a triennial review by the LEA

Appendix 4.1

Managing the Development of ICT in the Primary School

Questions to the researcher

(1) What aspects of your background experience helped in this research?

(2) How did you set about gathering a sample? How representative were the schools?

(3) One gets the impression that ICT posts demand status but are invariably linked to other core curriculum or key stage responsibilities; to what extent is that the case across the LEA?

(4) One of the main prompts for change appears to be an OFSTED inspection how much is this to do with the crisis change that Clarke (1994: 20) identifies?

(5) What evidence was there of support staff and other helpers in your sample? To what extent could they be utilised as an extra resource?

(6) What do you see as the main destabilising forces for schools as shown in the Smith and Langston (1999) model?

(7) Many writers refer to employees resisting social change. What examples did you find in your research, and in your work generally?

(8) Fullan's (1993) comment that 'educational change is technically simple and socially complex' appears at odds with ICT developments and the socially supportive networks many schools develop as coping strategies. Is this the case?

(9) Staying with Fullan and his views about teachers displaying a 'conservative mentality', to what extent is this determined by their commitment to improve the measurable i.e. literacy, numeracy and science, as evidence of what Bennet *et al.* (1992) refer to as matters of quality or delighting their customers, the government and parents?

(10) How much do the pre-conditions for implementing change lie with the LEA rather than individual schools?

(11) How could training be developed to an acceptable standard?

(12) Any other comments since your research.

References

Bennett, N., Crawford, M. and Riches, C. (1992) *Managing Change in Education*. Milton Keynes: Open University Press.
Blunkett, D. (2000) "Raising aspirations in the 21st century". Speech at North of England Conference. DfEE.
Clarke, L. (1994) *The Essence of Change*. London: Prentice Hall.
Drucker, P. (1993) *The Coming of the New Organisation*. Oxford: Butterworth and Heinemann.
Fullan, M. (1993) *Change Forces*. London: Falmer.
Leigh, A. (1994) *Effective Change*. London: IPM.

Smith, A. and Langston, A. (1999) *Managing Staff in Early Years Settings*. London: Routledge.

Smith, A. and Sykes, C. (2000) "Managing innovation and change in education". MA course programme, Edge Hill College of Higher Education.

Stewart, J. (1996) *Managing Change Through Training and Development*. London: Kogan Page.

Whitaker, P. (1993) *Managing Change in Schools*. Milton Keynes: Open University Press.

Chapter Five

Improving Development Planning in Primary Schools

WHEN first appointed as deputy head by a 'traditional' head-teacher Tricia Braddock found that her managerial involvement was somewhat limited. Roles and responsibilities largely precluded her from decision-making whilst any development planning was at best *ad hoc*. When a new headteacher was appointed things changed considerably for, with headship experience of two other schools, his style was more collaborative and open, particularly over policy and direction. One of his first decisions was to allow Braddock full responsibility for school development planning; a task some deputies would find too daunting. However as an established figure in the school and the community and having recently completed a postgraduate diploma in education management she felt confident in fulfilling that role. With over twenty years experience she has taught across the key stages and held a number of curriculum responsibilities including language, assessment, art and display, as well as being an early years co-ordinator. Furthermore she had the insight to chronicle in detail other schools' attempts at policy-making and strategic development in an area that still remains largely neglected.

In this respect, the performance of her own school was significant. Serving an area of predominantly local authority with some private housing, the school catchment area lacked the advantages of more affluent areas. Nevertheless, the open and welcoming approach, designed to gain the trust and views of parents, did much to break down barriers and increase participation by parents and the community. The use of performance data to monitor pupils and inform staff, together with target-setting, proved an integral factor in raising levels of achievement and overall improvement. As a result, the school's results grew consistently above what might be expected given the percentage eligible for free school meals (the accepted measure of socio-economic disadvantage). Braddock therefore was well placed to research other schools and their approach to developmental planning, something she undertook with the aid of three case studies linked to an overview of developments.

The Study

In the introduction to her research, Braddock stressed the importance of pupil achievement and the difference, through the quality of teaching and learning, that individual schools can make. Her arguments centred on systematic development and strategic planning, a term she defined as:

> focusing on the aims of education to bring together all aspects of school's planning and thereby turn long-term vision into short-term goals to give teachers more control over the nature and pace of change.

She believed that too few schools engaged in such careful analysis of needs and as a result often found themselves being led by external forces, something she traced back to the 1988 Education Reform Act. This Act, with its new boundaries of control and accountability, had significant implications for school development planning. Hence, despite the lack of legislation it cannot be coincidental that as far back as 1982, 98 per cent of schools were found to have had development plans in one form or another.

The precise format and approaches to planning provided an introduction to the key writers on school improvement (Hargreaves and Hopkins, 1994; Davies and Ellison, 1997; Dean, 1999). Amongst them there was a strong measure of agreement on the need for initial audits and consultation as a baseline starting point. This, together with creating the right climate and cultural norms, 'those values, procedures and expectations that guide people's behaviours within an organisation' (MacGilchrist *et al.*, 1995), was seen as essential if the school's capacity to manage improvement successfully were to be achieved. Setting aside the time element of at least three years, that Golstein and Thomas (1995) identified as being necessary to make judgements on performance data, the major aim of the school development planning is still often not translated into the classroom as MacGilchrist's research revealed:

> OFSTED reported that recent inspections had revealed that whilst in the primary schools the quality of school development plans had improved, monitoring and evaluating the standards of achievement and the quality of the work in the classroom was the most frequently neglected task.

Parallel to the impact on classroom performance identified by OFSTED lies the limited consultation and involvement of governors. According to Cuckle *et al.* (1998), far from helping provide an overview of what was required:

> The most that was said in several schools by governors and head-teachers alike was that governors 'could suggest items if they wanted'. It was also said by some headteachers that governors had never questioned what was in the SDP.

The effect of such short-sightedness provides an explanation as to why school development planning tends to address only the immediate needs of the organisation, as Knight (1997) illustrated:

> There is little evidence of serious analysis of probable alternative futures and consequently even less of structured exploration of possible options for responding to these.

A diametric view was offered by Davies and Ellison (1998) who compared strategic planning to a journey 'in which we are extrapolating patterns from the past and projecting forward in the future'. They argued that the premise of a predictable environment could no longer be accepted or, as Hamel and Prahalad (1989) described, 'the predictive horizon is becoming shorter and shorter'. Such has been the turbulence of recent years that many would argue for an incremental approach. However, this would have minimal impact on what Davies and Ellison termed the 'capability enhancement', a number of definable goals which could be benchmarked to measure individual progress as well as serving as a framework for evaluation and review. Weindling's (1997: 219) view of the process succinctly summarised what for many headteachers remains unmapped territory which they are reluctant to share with other stakeholders:

Strategic planning has as its key the notion of strategic thinking which considers the vision and values of the organisation as well as the anticipated external forces and trends which affect the school, to produce what might be called the 'helicopter view' ... Strategic planning is a means of establishing and maintaining a sense of direction when the future becomes more and more difficult to predict.

The Methodology

Braddock's use of interviews to support three case studies of local primary schools (see Figure 5.1 for a summary of the main characteristics of the three schools used) allowed her the opportunity to interpret patterns of behaviour that could be cross-referenced against other accounts recorded in the school. As a deputy headteacher she believed she was well placed, being neither threatening to co-ordinators nor over-awed by headteachers and chairs of governors. Her schedule of questions (see Appendix 5.1) focused on nine main areas supported by one or more supplementary questions. Each of the nine points was based on her literature review or, in the case of question 5, training and current issues in education. Whilst the schedules for headteacher and deputy were more or less identical (excepting the difference in role), questions for the co-ordinator were focused towards experience and curricular responsibility.

Although Braddock's case studies reflected the individual responses of the schools, space does not allow for a more detailed response. Instead, answers have been selected to provide a flavour of the research whilst at the same time retaining verbatim quotations.

Results and Analysis

The first five interview questions have been used to guide the reader up to question 5, which was on training, while other areas have been incorporated into the text.

School Development/Strategic Plan

Here, Braddock stated that she was particularly interested in the strategic planning element, agreeing with Fidler's (1996) arguments that existing headteachers needed to be introduced to the concept of strategy and a sense of strategic direction in a time when things were more and more difficult to predict. However, in School 1 both the headteacher and deputy asked for

Type and size of school	Staff	OFSTED comments	School Development Plan
School 1 Church of England primary Mixed background from urban area 280 on roll Premises 1973	H/T 2 hrs D/H 6 yrs	Good relationships within school but work of governing body underdeveloped.	OFSTED reported that the new SDP provided a framework of support to help the school improve. Funding implications are clearly indicated.
School 2 Community primary 415 on roll Urban area of mixed socio-economic background	H/T well established D/H 1 year exp.	1995 report highlighted need to review and extend the role of governors. 1998 inspection indicated this had now been addressed.	OFSTED viewed SDP as good, 'with governors taking an active part in producing and monitoring its success'. Subject co-ordinators praised for leadership and involved in development planning.
School 3 Community primary 450 on roll 80 per cent of Asian heritage Urban area of mixed socio-economic background	H/T 1 year D/H well established	1998 report commented on strong partnership with parents and the full involvement of the governing body.	OFSTED stated 'the school development plan is a useful, effective working document which addresses clearly laid out aims and objectives which are reflected in the daily life of the school'.

Figure 5.1:   Background to sample schools

clarification, indicating that they did not understand the difference between the two forms. Braddock quoted the headteacher, who suggested that:

> 'A school development plan is a much bigger document which contains all aspects of the school development, whilst a strategic plan focuses more on specific issues related to a tighter time scale.'

Meanwhile, in School 2 the deputy headteacher admitted that for her a strategic plan was a new idea. However, the deputy headteacher in School 3 offered a clearer view:

> 'The main aim is that you control events rather than school just reacting. We are trying to manage the change rather than letting the change manage us.'

Responses to Braddock's supplementary questions on development or strategic plans revealed other evidence of misunderstandings along with a belief that an all-inclusive approach was the answer, with one deputy head-teacher reporting:

> 'Every member of staff has prioritised something within their subject. She indicated that no school priorities had been identified.'

and another arguing that:

> 'We have always been very bad at pooling things in this profession ... and I think that if somebody comes up with a good pattern which everybody recognises as being manageable, then my fifty pages can go out of the window.'

The Aim/Purpose of a School Development/Strategic Plan

School 1 furnished a near textbook answer to this question, but both head-teacher and deputy omitted to mention the need to raise pupil achievement. A similar view was taken by the headteacher of School 2 who, when asked how the plan linked to pupil learning, indicated that the 'whole plan was geared towards improving the effectiveness of teaching and the quality of children's learning'. In School 3, the deputy headteacher outlined an approach designed to create more of an overview:

'The one we had before was simply a list of action that needed to be taken, the dates, who was doing it, the budget and how it would be evaluated. The one we have now actually tries to highlight which areas are ongoing, ready for review, when certain ones will be replaced. It's all colour coded so it is easier to spot when things need to be done and plan ahead.'

On the supplementary question of links with pupil learning/finance, School 1 indicated that the full financial position was made available in the front of the plan, including reserves and planned spending. Both the other schools referred to finance and the linking of the school development plan as part of the process to give priority to spending needs in the present climate.

Composition of School Development/Strategic Plan

Here there were some predictable responses. Some headteachers, as with School 1, listed their own headings of mission statement, aims, finance, admission, health and safety policies, school projects, staffing, curriculum, premises, community, and annual events. The deputy headteacher in School 2 thought that after consultation (with whom was not made clear) the plan would highlight several key aims and priorities to move the school forward.

'Our school development plan has every subject covered, at the previous school we didn't target more areas than about six. I'm not sure this works but I'm not saying the other one was perfect either. It covers things such as overall curriculum, behaviour and parental involvement.'

With the supplementary questions here centred around priorities and implementation, it was perhaps inevitable that the then recently announced numeracy hour would skew responses. At the same time issues generated by school inspection provided another example of externally-driven initiatives dominating the planning process. Information and communication technology and literacy were other key areas most likely to drive plans off course. A final supplementary question focused on implementation and monitoring, something that the headteacher of School 1 ensured took place through co-ordinators reporting back to governors, a view reiterated in School 3.

Staff Involvement in School Development/Strategic Planning

The interview schedule went on to explore the area of staff and governor participation, as well as the role of parents and community in planning. The deputy headteacher in School 1 spoke for many when he wished for greater involvement on his part:

'Yes, I would like to have a lot more input in school development planning. Firstly, I am applying for headship and it would be of good use to have actually done a plan in a constructive way over a period of time. Secondly, having been heavily involved in curriculum it is good to know where the curriculum is going. The key problem is time to do these things.'

Meanwhile, a long interregnum in School 2 had caused a re-definition of roles and subsequent reduction in expectations. However, the experienced deputy headteacher in School 3 admitted that even he did not have a specific input into development planning, a fact confirmed by the headteacher when she said that he was no more involved than other senior staff. For the co-ordinators there appeared to be a degree of participation, best summarised by School 2, where co-ordinators were seen individually by the headteacher to discuss plans and progress made.

It was evident from Braddock's questioning that parents played a minor role in the process, something that remained a key feature in her own school and generated prompting a somewhat loaded question. Once again the reactions of senior staff were lukewarm as encapsulated by the deputy headteacher of School 1:

'I would probably see too many disadvantages, you're going to get a real range of views of where the school should be going to and we can't satisfy all those opinions, by doing some you will make others dissatisfied. I think … the school needs to go in its own direction for the children's benefit and not for the parents.'

Similarly, the headteacher of School 2 claimed that he was too busy to undertake a parental survey, although his deputy conceded that there would be an element of consultation with parents over personal and social educational issues as well as citizenship. However, ultimately it would be the staff who decided. In the case of School 3, responses implied a 'take-it or leave-it' attitude. Ultimately there was some parental consultation on individual matters (no examples given) and if parents were unhappy about anything they had the names and addresses of the governors.

Fortunately such a state of affairs did not appear to extend to governors, largely one suspects due to the influence of OFSTED inspections (see Figure 5.1). Here, Braddock's decision to interview the chair or vice chair of governors proved an insightful one, particularly in the case of the first school, where the chair of governors was a former business analyst and currently systems manager of a large company. He offered his services to the headteacher and over eighteen months created a database for target setting. When the school adviser next visited he was impressed with the whole school English results being plotted on a spreadsheet. The only criticism, however, was that the targets were below County expectations which could lead to allegations of being a failing school. At this point the governor replied, 'Hang on a minute, you said set your targets and we set our targets and now you're saying because we met them we are failing, so why don't you just impose the targets?', going on to demonstrate the whole process of identifying potential which was quite intense and continuous and involved looking at every child. When the adviser saw the depth of analysis he agreed and simply asked only for the PIPs data to be added as well.

Further evidence of governors' seriousness and weight of responsibility was given by another interviewee when he referred to sourcing other highly acclaimed school development plans as a vehicle for discussion at future meetings. By contrast, the chair of governors of School 3, despite six years in post, still appeared very much at the margins of decision-making and policy. Whilst Braddock's diplomacy and tact prevented her from excessive probing, nevertheless an impression emerged of only moderate involvement, supplemented by a high level of respect for professional expertise and autonomy. One explanation referred to the lack of recent training undertaken in this area, the subject of question 5.

Staff Training in School Development Planning

Responses here went some way to explaining the steep learning curve needed if full participation were to be achieved. The most up-to-date appeared to be School 1 where the headteacher's previous experience held her in good stead. In the same school the curriculum co-ordinator spoke in glowing terms of a recent local education authority management case and how training for all staff would be valuable as:

'I think a lot of people feel it is just something else to do and they don't have an understanding or overview of it. I think training in understanding of its purpose would make it more successful.'

Yet in the same school management team was the deputy headteacher who admitted he needed to upgrade his knowledge, whilst the governor interviewed was very critical of recent numeracy training, believing the focus should have been on how governors could support the headteacher and school in the numeracy hour. Such levels of involvement contrast sharply with School 2 where neither the headteacher nor staff had had any recent training in school development planning. The only exception appeared to be the governor who stressed the importance of school development plans, along with the need to make some kind of annual training event attractive to governors. Such comments were largely echoed by School 3 where the headteacher reported a positive response from OFSTED with regard to her planning documents some three years earlier. However, the lack of training for the deputy headteacher and co-ordinator over the previous seven to eight years, as well as governors' absence, appeared a serious weakness.

Reflections on the Study

Despite the small sample, Braddock appears to have recorded many of the key features of primary school development planning as well as identifying several areas for concern. First, the area would appear to be characterised by a lack of knowledge and misunderstandings by senior staff to an extent that would not be countenanced over curriculum or teaching issues. A measure of blame for this must be apportioned to the local education authority, although obviously OFSTED needs to adopt a stronger role in identifying such weaknesses.

Second, staff involvement was at best patchy with once again deputy headteachers appearing to play a largely unfulfilled role in proceedings. This area of school management parallels in places the secret garden of the 1960s with legitimate stakeholders of parents and governors being kept at arms length. In some schools this extended to teachers whilst the evidence of support staff involvement was even more limited.

Third, there is a danger that development planning is used as a holdall for all future school events rather than being subject to sound analysis and priority. All of this leads us to the question of training and development for staff and other interested parties. Once again what stood out was the paucity of some professionals' experiences through no fault of their own. Often they saw themselves marginalised through the demands of full time class teaching yet conscious of the need to upgrade knowledge through visits to other schools and courses of study. Hence, the example of the governor in School 2 who obtained materials from other schools is to be commended. Thankfully he is not alone in undertaking his responsibilities so seriously as the extract from the interview with the governor in School 1 confirmed. In response to a final question he referred back to strategic planning, stating:

> 'I'm not sure whether strategic planning is the right way to go in a school of our size … working where I work now in further education I can see the benefits of a strategic plan, our strategic plan takes us up to the year 2003, but I can't see how that would benefit a school. I think the environment is so volatile that you may end up struggling to forward plan because things change.'

Such a comment is worthy of note, highlighting issues explored in Davies and Ellison's (1998) research. Nevertheless, it would be wrong to accept this as an excuse for what has been shown to be clear underperformance and involvement in such a key area of school improvement.

Recommendations

- Deputy headteachers to become more involved in school development planning
- In-service training for governors on school development plan issues
- Local education authorities to support local forums to discuss strategic planning issues
- Co-ordinators to report on development planning to governors on an annual basis

Appendix 5.1

Interview Schedule (Headteacher)

(1)   Does your school have a school development/strategic plan?

    S1   How often is it written?

    S2   How did you decide on the present format of the plan?

    S3   What in your view is the difference between a strategic plan and a school development plan?

    S4   What are the advantages/disadvantages of having a strategic plan rather than a SDP?

    S5   Would you consider drawing up a strategic plan? Why?

(2)   What in your view is the aim/purpose of school development/strategic plan?

    S1   In what ways does your plan link with pupil learning/finance?

(3)   What in your view should a good school development/strategic plan consist of? Why?

    S2   What are your priorities for the coming school year? How were they selected?

    S3   How do you ensure the plan is implemented and remains on schedule?

(4)   In what ways do you involve your staff in school development/strategic planning?

    S1   What role does the deputy play in terms of his/her management role?

    S2   What role do curriculum co-ordinators play in terms of planning for their areas?

    S3   How are staff involved in each stage of the process (setting targets, implementation, review and evaluation)?

(5)   Have you or any of your staff had any recent training in this area?

    S1   Outline briefly any internal/external training you have had and evaluate its usefulness.

    S2   What training do you think would be useful for yourself/your staff?

(6)   In what ways do you involve the governors in school development/strategic planning?

    S1   What do you consider are the advantages/disadvantages of involving the governors?

    S2   Have any of your governors had any recent training in this area?

    S3   Who provided the training?

S4   What impact do you feel this had on school development planning in the school?

S5   What do you feel needs to be done to improve governor involvement in this area in your school?

(7)   In what ways do you involve parents in school development/strategic planning?

S1   What in your view are the advantages/disadvantages of involving parents in school development planning?

(8)   Who monitors and evaluates the plan and how often is this undertaken?

(9)   Is there anything else you would like to add in terms of school development/ strategic planning?

References

Cuckle, P., Dunford, J., Hodgson, J. and Broadhead, P. (1998) "Governor involvement in development planning: from tea parties to working parties", *School Leadership and Management*, 18, (1), 19-33.

Davies, B. and Ellison, L. (1998) "Strategic planning in schools: an oxymoron?", *School Leadership and Management*, 18, (4), 461-73.

Davies, B. and Ellison, L. (1997) *School Development Planning*. Harlow: Longman.

Dean, J. (1999) *Improving the Primary School*. London: Routledge.

Goldstein, H. and Thomas, S. (1995) "School effectiveness and value added analysis", *Forum*, 37, (2), 36-8.

Hamel, G. and Prahalad, C.K. (1989) *The Empowered School: The Management and Practice of School Development Planning*. London: Cassell.

Hargreaves, D.H. and Hopkins, D. (eds.) (1994) *Development Planning for School Improvement*. London: Cassell.

Knight, J. (1997) *Strategic Planning for School Managers*. London: Kogan Page.

MacGilchrist, B., Mortimore, P., Savage, J. and Beresford, C. (1995) *Planning Matters: The Impact of Development Planning in Primary Schools*. London: Chapman.

Weindling, D. (1997) "Strategic planning in schools" in M. Preedy, R. Glatter and R. Levacic (eds.) *Educational Management: Strategy, Quality and Resources*. Milton Keynes: Open University Press.

Chapter Six

Effective Leadership Behaviour
in Primary Schools

I T was the move from his position as deputy headteacher into his present post as a primary school headteacher that prompted Keith Parkinson to undertake a study into effective actions and approaches to leadership in primary education. He has many years of experience of leadership in education, comprising six as a deputy headteacher and considerable time spent managing other areas of responsibility in schools.

The literature review he produced for his investigation demonstrated a sophisticated appreciation of writing in areas of both leadership and effectiveness, leading to an impressive synthesis of the two. Parkinson concluded from his reading that effective schools are those that satisfy a range of effectiveness criteria; that leadership is not enough without effective management; and that it is possible to identify leadership behaviours that can be considered effective or ineffective.

Background to the Research

There is currently a great deal of official attention being paid to educational leadership. The establishment of the National College for School Leadership and the training programmes available for both aspiring headteachers and those already in post, reflect a growing commitment to this area. Drucker (1992) reminded us that leadership is a means and not an end in itself. This truth is evident throughout this research. Leadership is identified as part of the mechanism used in schools to achieve goals and a major force in a school's culture. Parkinson was convinced from evidence in the literature that effective leadership has positive effects on pupil outcomes and thus endeavoured to discover the extent to which the ingredients of effective leadership were present and how they were experienced in a number of primary schools.

An effective leader is argued to have a vision for the school; strategies for achieving the vision, that are inclusive; and the means to communicate these to all staff. Hence, the personal actions of the leader are crucial. A transformational leadership style (Angus, 1989) that is educative (Evers, 1992), ethical (Foster, 1989) and authentic (Marks and Louis, 1997), is the model that underpinned this study and was evaluated. This values-based management philosophy was summarised (Bhindi and Duignan, 1997: 119) as one

> based on personal integrity and credibility, trusting relationship and commitment to ethical and moral values. Leaders *earn* their allegiance through authentic actions and interactions in trusting relationships, and through the shaping of organisational structures, processes and practices that enshrine authentic values and standards. (Original italics)

Parkinson believed that the thoughts, beliefs and values of the head-teacher enacted in his or her behaviour could have a profound impact on the effectiveness of the school through the way it influenced the actions, attitudes and motivation of others:

> Where staff management is skilled and sympathetic, a successful organisation is likely to result. Where it is clumsy and inadequate, poor performance may occur. (Bush and Middlewood, 1997: 11)

The Study

The central purpose of the research was to determine the link between leadership behaviour and effectiveness. It is not possible to correlate quantitative indicators of effectiveness, such as assessment results, with qualitative data about leadership in a small-scale project. Parkinson was interested in investigating perceptions of leader behaviour and how this in turn affects morale, motivation, commitment and behaviour of teachers. Where these are affected negatively, it is reasonable to assume, the conditions for school effectiveness are not met.

Two research methods, questionnaire (see Appendix 6.1) and semi-structured interview (see Appendix 6.2), were selected: the questionnaire, to allow use of a larger sample with an easily collated and interpreted range of data; the interview, to encourage responses in greater depth. Both the questionnaire and interview schedule were piloted.

The questionnaire asked for opinions on and actual occurrence of:

- participative management;
- support for staff;
- vision;
- strategic management;
- staff development and communication.

This made it possible to group the answers for analysis. The interview questions explored the same themes. The 'master' questionnaire used initials to indicate the analysis group the item belonged to. This was not a feature on the questionnaires sent out to teachers.

The Sample

The sample for the questionnaires comprised all willing members of staff in ten primary schools. The choice of schools predicted a significant return as the headteachers were known to the researcher. The questionnaires were coded by school and information sought regarding the role of the teacher completing it. Respondents were asked if they would be willing to be interviewed.

For the interviews three respondents from each of three schools were chosen. These represented a cross-section of teachers, including headteachers, senior managers and standard scale teachers. Parkinson supplied all the schools with non-attributable raw data from the questionnaires because he believed it to be important to disseminate research data. This may have inhibited some schools, that identified themselves as scoring negatively, from taking part in the interviews. The three schools selected from the original sample, however, did present as wide a range of leadership styles as it was possible to identify from the initial analysis of the survey.

Results and Analysis

School	Question Groups							
	P %	S %	E %	C %	SD %	V %	SM %	School Mean %
1	64.0	67.7	71.9	62.0	85.0	78.6	80.6	72.8
2	67.2	67.7	81.8	67.4	90.5	93.3	97.2	80.7
3	55.2	64.1	52.1	46.9	48.1	63.5	87.5	59.6
4	61.0	78.9	79.6	77.4	81.0	96.7	96.3	81.6
5	38.1	47.4	65.0	25.0	29.6	96.4	63.6	52.2
6	Only one respondent – no analysis made							
7	61.4	85.7	91.7	96.9	96.6	97.5	95.9	89.4
8	68.9	75.7	91.8	61.4	83.9	92.1	100	82.0
9	70.5	70.9	96.5	80.0	78.7	98.3	85.7	82.9
10	51.7	44.8	44.5	41.7	76.2	66.7	66.7	56.0
Mean	61.5	70.4	78.8	64.8	77.0	88.3	98.8	

P = Participation in Decision-Making
S = Support for Staff
E = Expectations
C = Communication
SD = Staff Development
V = Vision
SM = Strategic Management

Figure 6.1:   Individual school figures – percentage of positive responses by question group

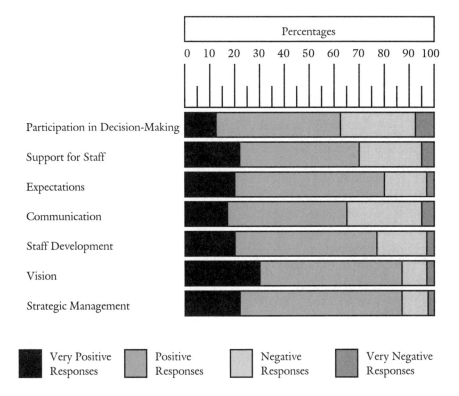

Figure 6.2:   Group analysis graph

A largely positive picture emerged from the results of the questionnaires as figures 6.1 and 6.2 above show.

Questionnaires

Primary school teachers perceived many of the identified features of effective leadership taking place in their schools. However, there were differences in the degree to which the different features were apparent. Across all question areas there were more positives than negatives, with evidence for leadership strengths lying more in the areas of vision and strategic management than in participative decision-making and communication. Headteachers were clear in the main about the direction they wanted for the school and were also clear about how they could achieve this. This indicated that they were less effective in what have been termed as transformational, educative or ethical elements, in which empowerment is an important feature. Parkinson suggested, on the basis of the evidence, that headteachers may be reluctant to entrust their vision to the staff.

The other aspects of leadership were positively upheld in the survey. The majority of respondents felt they were led supportively and that there were clear expectations and opportunities for staff development.

Parkinson explored the pattern of responses in individual schools, urging caution in putting too much weight on the evidence as the sample in each school was usually only four or five respondents. (School 6 was not referred to at all in this context, as there was only one response.) However, this section of the analysis of results provided some interesting comparisons and variations.

All the schools conformed generally with the overall pattern, although schools 2 and 4 were the only ones to fit it exactly. One interesting comparison was the level of scoring. Schools 8 and 9 scored high positive responses in all areas, whereas in contrast School 3 produced a significantly lower number of positive responses. It is clear that even where leaders have similar strengths and weaknesses, within the general pattern there are varying degrees to which positive aspects of effective leadership are perceived.

Only schools 3, 5, and 10 produced overall negative responses to some questions. School 3 scored fewer than 50 per cent positive responses to questions relating to communication and staff development. School 10 attracted similarly negative scores for support for staff, expectations and, lowest of all, communication. The position in School 5 was even more dramatic with the areas of participation, support for staff, communication and staff development all scoring an overall negative response.

Once again it is the aspects related to transformative leadership that are experienced as weak, suggesting a lack of involvement and trust of staff. Spaulding (1997) identified headteacher behaviours which had negative consequences for teacher development and behaviour:

> lack of participatory decision making; lack of support; showing favouritism; unclear/unreasonable expectations; flexing muscle; micromanaging; and contradictory body language.

Parkinson examined the range of scores overall, for each question group and for each school. This analysis revealed interesting variations. Schools 1, 2, 4, 7, 8 and 9 had similar ranges to the overall pattern, set at a comparable level.

School 1 provided the smallest range, being close to the overall range although the distribution was different. School 7's relatively low score of 61.4 per cent for participative decision-making increased the range, thus masking very high scoring in all other aspects. The next lowest score was 85.7 per cent for support for staff. These schools' statistics suggested a balance of leadership behaviour that was responded to in a positive manner. The widest range came from School 5. A range of 71.4 per cent was produced, from a 25 per cent score for communication to a highest 96.4 per cent score for vision. This picture was further unbalanced as the nearest high score was 65 per cent for expectations. Where there are very strong ideas about the direction of the school, less strength in strategic management of that vision, with weaknesses in the ability to communicate and lead staff towards achieving it, there are indications of an unbalanced leadership approach.

Interviews

Interviews were conducted in schools 1, 5 and 7 to investigate the above findings in more depth. From the questionnaire data School 1 represented a typical example, School 7 was reported as highly effective, whilst School 5 appeared to lack some ingredients for effectiveness.

In School 7 all the staff had been in the school for a long time, including the deputy headteacher who had taught in the school for twenty-three years. The headteacher had a total of three years in that leadership role and had previously been deputy there for six years. The interviews at School 1 reflected both past and present practice as the headteacher was just coming to the end of his first year in post and was attempting to implement a very different decision-making regime from the other, long-established staff had been used to. Parkinson conjectured that this situation might have accounted for some of the mixed messages from the interviews. The headteacher of School 5 had been in post five years. The interviews and questionnaires from staff there reflected unfavourably on almost all aspects of leadership, particularly participation and communication. The headteacher openly admitted that she had recently returned from the qualifications and curriculum authority (QCA) leadership course inspired. She had begun to use her reflections on this and the raw data from the questionnaires to make changes to her approach. Therefore her interview reflected situations that she had identified for change or had begun to change.

Participative Decision-Making

Participative decision-making scored fewest positive responses from School 5 and second fewest in schools 1 and 7. There appeared to be a predominance of decision-making by the headteacher and senior management teams. From the questionnaires, school development planning appeared to be almost exclusive to the headteacher in School 7, whereas from the other two schools there were mixed responses, suggesting more involvement. When this was explored in the interviews, there emerged a more varied picture in all the schools. In all three cases the originator of school development priorities seemed to be the headteacher, sometimes with senior managers. However, in all schools there were opportunities, which operated in different ways, for staff to contribute. In School 5, a formalised structure was described by the school management team:

> 'Each co-ordinator decides what needs doing in the coming year or longer term. We share that altogether in the staff meeting, it's discussed and that basically – what we decided – is done during the year.'

In School 7 there remained throughout the interviews an agreement that decision-making was the prerogative of the headteacher. There did appear, however, to be significant indirect involvement by staff. Where staff did feel able to express their perceptions of need, a sensitive information-gathering process was in place. A number of channels communicated these to the school management team and even after decisions had been made they might be amended at staff meetings:

> 'We discuss and then he puts what he thinks forward ... He then puts it to the staff ... staff are involved in changing it as they wish ... All school issues are done this way.' (School 7, deputy headteacher)

School 1 presented contradictions. The headteacher claimed a 'collegiate style' and described involvement of staff in decision-making:

> 'I don't think I have all the answers to everything, I don't believe I do, so I want other people to come in and say, "that's what I think should happen".'

This was not the perception of the other staff interviewed who claimed that the school development plan was drawn up and presented to the staff with little, or no staff contribution to the process.

Respondents generally felt that staff meetings were forums for decision-making and that they had a voice. There was consultation and decision-making by staff on operational rather than strategic issues. It became apparent that staff members had involvement through delegated tasks and responsibilities. One headteacher, for example, disagreed with the choice of book supplier made by a co-ordinator but did not interfere, as responsibility for that decision had been delegated. However, when it came to bigger issues relating to curriculum, the participation in decision-making was there limited to a very narrow range. Senior management teams made all the major decisions in the three schools. This was a source of confusion for some staff who were unclear about the role and functions of these bodies. Below is a fairly typical example, in answer to the prompt 'How does the senior management team work?':

'I've no idea. I presume they just meet and make the decisions and then tell the rest of us.' (School 5, newly qualified teacher)

Questions relating to curriculum policy-writing revealed that there was a tendency for co-ordinators to work on policies individually and then present them to staff, sometimes for limited discussion. A phrase common to all the headteachers was 'I don't like presenting people with a blank page'. There was little evidence that teachers thought it should be any other way:

'Sometimes decisions have to be made and they'll always be unpopular and I think it's the head's role to say that a decision has to be made.' (School 7, standard scale teacher)

Headteachers and some staff went to great lengths to explain what they considered to be an 'appropriate' level of involvement. The staff in School 5 felt strongly, in both the questionnaires and interviews, that there was not enough participation and called for joint decision-making. Staff in School 1 reported an increase in this approach throughout the year, leading to greater effectiveness.

'Staff are included more, decisions made as a whole staff. This makes more effectiveness because everyone is informed, people know what's happening and it's a better learning atmosphere.' (School 1, allowance holder)

Hallinger *et al.* (1993: 33) found that teachers 'favoured a more active role in decision-making' while managers 'tended to question the numbers of teachers who wanted to participate'. In each of the schools the head-teachers recognised the value of participation in decision-making, yet were wrestling with the practicalities of how much and how to organise it:

> ... the perennial challenge of establishing and sustaining a balance between on the one hand, control of the organisation and, on the other, staff participation and involvement. (Hall and Southworth, 1997: 165)

There was also the fear that to relinquish some decision-making might dilute the vision. The headteacher in School 1 recounted a range of manipulative techniques to control decisions that he employed to encourage staff to believe that they have been prime movers. The deputy headteacher of School 7 also saw that involvement was a motivator, yet seemed cynical of the process:

> 'It's effective because if they haven't been involved they won't implement it properly ... they'll put a bit more effort in, therefore it's better for the children – it's bluffing really.'

These examples call into question the authenticity of behaviour and ignore the spirit in which Fullan and Hargreaves (1992: 121) offered this proposition:

> Heads who share authority and establish conditions conducive to empowerment, actually *increase* their influence over what is accomplished in the school, as they work with staff to bring about improvement. (Original italics)

Communication

From the questionnaires communication was another area that seemed weak, although this impression was not generally upheld in the interviews.

In all the schools where interviews took place, systems for keeping teachers informed were in place. These included staff meetings, calendars and notice boards. Staff in schools 1 and 7 were very satisfied with the effectiveness of measures to inform in their schools.

School 5 was an exception to this level of satisfaction. The headteacher spoke of calendars of events but did not seem to consider communication as anything other than telling people about operational situations. The newly qualified teacher interviewed confirmed that the school had few formal communication systems but also described how the early-years co-ordinator kept all Key Stage 1 staff informed. This co-ordinator, who was in a better position to appreciate the change of approach the headteacher was working towards, was also interviewed. When asked about communication, she too acknowledged that it was poor and believed that the frustration caused lead to stressed teachers unable to work effectively in the classroom. However, she commented favourably on the increasing improvement which was taking place in this area. Previously the headteacher had been unable to implement effective communication in the school, affecting the overall effectiveness of the school. As the newly qualified teacher put it, 'It's not as good a team as it should be'.

Communication systems that take full account of the needs of non-teaching staff were not found. They did not attend staff meetings nor necessarily have a base where written communication could be left. There was no awareness of the need to establish channels of communication. In the case of classroom assistants there was a tacit understanding that the teachers working most closely with them would pass on relevant information.

Similarly there emerged no appreciation of the need to disseminate information from senior management team discussion of governors' meetings. The headteachers in schools 5 and 7, who had not previously thought this important, as a result of the question, took steps to address these aspects of communication. The importance was demonstrated in an example cited by the headteacher of School 1, speaking about the aftermath of a senior management team meeting:

'The mistake I made was that I didn't tell everybody that this was the discussion that was going on, and not that there was a secret about it, but there appeared to be a secret, and there was a bit of insecurity, not insecurity, uncertainty.' (School 1, headteacher)

The importance of good communication was recognised by those in the sample and overall judged to be effective. Good communication was apparently reflected in the morale of the staff and their effectiveness:

'Impact on children? ... if staff are aware of what is happening and where children should be it helps discipline.' (School 1, allowance holder)

Communication appeared from the interviews to be understood mainly in terms of the success or otherwise of top-down, information-giving. Parkinson has already provided evidence that questions the strength of systems to consult staff and engage them in the decision-making process. It is possible that the discrepancy between the weakness of communication reported in the questionnaires and the satisfaction expressed in the majority of interviews arises from a narrow interpretation of communication, by interviewees, that does not stray beyond acceptance of the need for timely operational information. It falls far short of Grace's (1995: 55) view:

The educative leader attempts to establish the conditions for dialogue, participation and respect for persons and their ideas.

Vision and Strategic Management

Vision and strategic management were indicated as areas of relative strength in the questionnaires. In the three schools where interviews took place they were highly placed. In School 5 they were placed first and second but with a wide discrepancy between the high score for vision and that for strategic management.

Parkinson found vision a difficult concept for respondents to discuss in an interview. He observed that people find it hard to express without resorting to clichéd or flowery language that might cause embarrassment. Because of this he chose to ask about the two aspects of vision and strategic management together in his questioning, by exploring the steps taken to implement the vision. Three different pictures emerged. In School 1 the uncertainties surrounding the first year of headship were revealed in the marked inconsistency of responses. The headteacher declared:

'I want to raise standards. The OFSTED report was good. I'm very aware that the next one has to be better than good – and it can be.'

This was endorsed by one of the other respondents:

> 'Difficult to see where we are going – with so many changes. The new head has different ideas and approaches.' (School 1, allowance holder)

but there was confusion expressed by another response.

Neither expressed the over-riding ingredient of the vision strongly argued by the headteacher, that of promoting the interests of the children with everything else, including recognition of staff needs, behind that.

In School 1 no clear answer was expressed concerning implementation of the vision. The headteacher, however, was able to recount anecdotal evidence of how he created opportunities to promote the vision, and how he manipulated discussions to give him the opportunity to challenge un-helpful relationships that might present a barrier to advancing it. Parkinson thus described a situation where there was leadership vision, supported by a strategic management approach. However, he indicated that this was not fully communicated throughout the school, suggesting that this could be a result of recency in post.

The questionnaires gave a positive response to questions on vision and strategic management in School 7. An impression was formed of a school with a clear direction and an understanding of how to get there, and this was borne out in the interviews. It was however expressed in practical terms rather than revealing an underlying philosophy. The headteacher felt it was not possible, in the current educational climate of external change, to hold a steady long-term vision. He did then proceed to speak of preparing children for a highly technical future and the need therefore to provide staff development for ICT. He also believed it was necessary to be reflective and self-critical as a school to ensure that the needs of the children continued to be met. His colleagues referred to the headteacher's drive as both forward-looking and thinking. The deputy headteacher commented: 'He's treading warily but he has plans for the next ten years.' These other interviewees described clearly the strategies adopted to implement the vision clearly and in some detail. Here the headteacher had been in senior management positions in the school for a total of nine years. Parkinson suggested this could have a bearing on the shared understanding of the vision and strategy. Communication was highly rated in the school and this also seemed important.

Once again on these aspects there were inconsistencies revealed in School 5. The imbalance between vision and strategic management that emerged in the questionnaires came across strongly in the interviews. Vision seemed most clearly articulated by the headteacher of School 5:

'What I would hope is that anyone who was working here was working on the basis that there is … no limit to what a child can achieve given the right circumstances. Just because we are in [an] area like this does not mean that we cannot do as well as people from other areas.'

This vision however had become communicated to other staff as being exclusively about results and not about children. One respondent described exhortations to improve and set targets without any discussion or direction about how this was to be achieved. When probed the headteacher revealed an apparent lack of awareness of how to achieve her vision for the school. She mentioned statistical sources of information such as PANDAS and SATS results but was vague about how they could be used.

Here leadership seemed less effective as the vision was poorly communicated and not supported by a clear strategy for action.

While possession of a vision, particularly one causing them to place emphasis on curriculum, teaching and learning and on care, appears crucial in the innovatory strategy of principals, it is significant that it is underpinned by an even wider vision; one which provides consistency, strength and coherence. (Dimmock and O'Donoghue, 1997: 150)

Expectations, Support for Staff, and Staff Development

From the questionnaire evidence these areas appeared to be strong features of primary schools. For leadership to create the right conditions for change, Northfield (1992: 96) argued:

There must be: opportunities to allow participants to develop personal understandings; opportunities to form social groups to allow for mutual support during the change process; and encouragement to reflect on practice.

High scores for expectations appeared to be related to high scores for vision in the schools where staff were interviewed. There also emerged a strongly expressed professionalism. As one respondent stated: 'As professionals we know what we expect of ourselves.'

High scores for support and staff development could be read as indicators of transformative or ethical leadership. Two of the headteachers thought staff would go to them with difficulties; the other acknowledged that staff had other networks of mutual support. In fact, in all the schools, departmental and friendship networks were a first resort. Perhaps teachers were more prepared to talk to the headteachers in two of the schools, being more confident that they would receive the support that they needed. The key issue seems not to be whether the headteacher was approachable, but whether a culture of mutual support and co-operation had been established.

Classroom assistants do not share the same level of opportunities for development. However, Parkinson did find evidence that this had begun to change with the introduction of the literacy and numeracy strategies, suggesting that this was vital in order to build effective teams and foster inclusiveness. This was the aim of the headteacher of School 1 which scored highest on this aspect. Parkinson believed that this was partly as a result of a new headteacher's eagerness to raise the level of staff involvement.

Ethical and educative leadership values individuals' contributions and recognises their rights to staff development. Evidence of commitment to staff development was for Parkinson an indicator of effective leadership. From the schools studied in depth, the one displaying fewest characteristics of effective leadership had strongly negative responses for staff development from the questionnaire. In this school emphasis was unswervingly on school needs, whereas a wider understanding of the effects on staff motivation and morale was indicated where a balance was established between individual and school needs in the other two schools.

Reflections on the Study

Despite encouraging evidence of effective leadership in the primary schools surveyed, Parkinson's findings echoed powerfully those of Fullan and Hargreaves (1992: 111) in their detailed analysis:

> Heads who control all decisions, who obstruct initiative, who choose blame before praise, who see only problems where others see possibilities, are heads who create discouraged and dispirited teachers.

Where headteachers demonstrated a genuine belief in whole staff involvement because it was right, rather than simply an effective approach, there was evidence of higher staff morale and motivation. A sense of shared purpose was established and the relevance of school management to school improvement was perceived. In cases where there were lower levels of effective communication, inefficiency and lack of focused team-working were experienced.

Where there were differences, these were sometimes in different aspects, but a general overall pattern emerged. Schools tended to score relatively well or relatively poorly in relation to the general pattern. Head-teachers had strong ideas about where schools should move to but weaker ones about how to get there. Communication and, therefore, successful implementation, of the vision was hampered by a number of identified factors.

Schools were affected by their staffing histories. They were also constantly responding to external educational expectations and change. Whilst displaying a measure of agreement about effective leadership that is transformative in approach, schools were working to change, adapt and develop management structures, procedures and understandings to balance each person's contribution. All this leads to further questions:

- What level of staff participation in decision-making is appropriate in relation to workload?
- What needs to change in primary schools to develop skilled and sympathetic leadership?
- Parkinson asserts that there is a strong relationship between effective leadership and school improvement. How can this link be experienced and evidenced?

Recommendations

- An examination of management roles of staff with responsibilities
- An examination of the expectations of all staff in relation to participative decision-making
- Regular review of communication channels by a sub-group of the whole staff and other stakeholders

Appendix 6.1

Master Questionnaire – School Reference

In this school:

P	Staff are asked for their opinions	Strongly agree	Agree	Disagree	Strongly disagree
S	The head is there to help in the classroom	Strongly agree	Agree	Disagree	Strongly disagree
E	Staff progress is reviewed against expectations	Strongly agree	Agree	Disagree	Strongly disagree
C	Staff are told about senior management discussions	Strongly agree	Agree	Disagree	Strongly disagree
M	The head understands how to put plans into action	Strongly agree	Agree	Disagree	Strongly disagree
D	There are regular opportunities for staff to discuss their development needs	Strongly agree	Agree	Disagree	Strongly disagree
P	The head writes the SDP	Strongly agree	Agree	Disagree	Strongly disagree
S	If a teacher has classroom problems the head will deal with the situation supportively	Strongly agree	Agree	Disagree	Strongly disagree
C	Staff expect to be told about decisions which affect them	Strongly agree	Agree	Disagree	Strongly disagree
V	The head motivates people to improve	Strongly agree	Agree	Disagree	Strongly disagree
E	Staff understand their roles	Strongly agree	Agree	Disagree	Strongly disagree
D	There are in-school training opportunities	Strongly agree	Agree	Disagree	Strongly disagree
P	Staff meetings result in real decision making	Strongly agree	Agree	Disagree	Strongly disagree
S	Children's behaviour in class is the class teacher's responsibility	Strongly agree	Agree	Disagree	Strongly disagree
C	Staff know what is going on in the school as a whole	Strongly agree	Agree	Disagree	Strongly disagree

V	The staff work towards developing the school ethos	Strongly agree	Agree	Disagree	Strongly disagree
M	The head reflects on patterns to help with decision-making	Strongly agree	Agree	Disagree	Strongly disagree
E	Staff are clear about what is expected from them	Strongly agree	Agree	Disagree	Strongly disagree
D	Staff are made aware of promotion opportunities	Strongly agree	Agree	Disagree	Strongly disagree
P	Staff feel reluctant to express their opinions	Strongly agree	Agree	Disagree	Strongly disagree
C	Staff are kept informed about governors' decisions	Strongly agree	Agree	Disagree	Strongly disagree
V	The staff understand and share the vision for the school	Strongly agree	Agree	Disagree	Strongly disagree
M	The head anticipates future problems or opportunities	Strongly agree	Agree	Disagree	Strongly disagree
D	Help is available for staff applying for jobs in other schools	Strongly agree	Agree	Disagree	Strongly disagree
P	Co-ordinators write policies and schemes of work and then show the staff	Strongly agree	Agree	Disagree	Strongly disagree
S	The head will help with a dispute with a parent	Strongly agree	Agree	Disagree	Strongly disagree
C	Staff are kept in the dark about senior management decisions	Strongly agree	Agree	Disagree	Strongly disagree
V	The head perseveres if he or she feels that the actions are in the best interests of the pupils, despite opposition	Strongly agree	Agree	Disagree	Strongly disagree
P	Long-term planning is done as a whole staff	Strongly agree	Agree	Disagree	Strongly disagree
S	Performance feedback is given positively	Strongly agree	Agree	Disagree	Strongly disagree
C	Decisions which affect staff are fully explained to them	Strongly agree	Agree	Disagree	Strongly disagree
V	The head cultivates an ethos of care and respect	Strongly agree	Agree	Disagree	Strongly disagree
D	Staff have opportunities to attend courses	Strongly agree	Agree	Disagree	Strongly disagree

P	Staff feel they make important decisions	Strongly agree	Agree	Disagree	Strongly disagree
S	The head lets staff know how they are doing	Strongly agree	Agree	Disagree	Strongly disagree
E	The head refuses to accept second best for the children	Strongly agree	Agree	Disagree	Strongly disagree
D	Staff are reluctant to inform the head that they are applying for jobs elsewhere	Strongly agree	Agree	Disagree	Strongly disagree
P	Decisions are made by the head and the school management team	Strongly agree	Agree	Disagree	Strongly disagree
S	The head will be sympathetic with personal problems which affect staff performance	Strongly agree	Agree	Disagree	Strongly disagree
V	Staff work in opposition to the head's vision for the school	Strongly agree	Agree	Disagree	Strongly disagree
V	The head encourages pride in the school from everyone	Strongly agree	Agree	Disagree	Strongly disagree
P	The opinions of the staff are valued	Strongly agree	Agree	Disagree	Strongly disagree
S	Staff believe that if they ring in sick the head will be annoyed	Strongly agree	Agree	Disagree	Strongly disagree
M	The head takes short, medium and long-term view	Strongly agree	Agree	Disagree	Strongly disagree
P	The staff help with school development planning	Strongly agree	Agree	Disagree	Strongly disagree
E	Expectations are expressed positively	Strongly agree	Agree	Disagree	Strongly disagree
C	The systems for keeping people informed are inefficient	Strongly agree	Agree	Disagree	Strongly disagree
V	The school ethos reflects the school's stated mission or aims	Strongly agree	Agree	Disagree	Strongly disagree
S	The head helps in class when needed	Strongly agree	Agree	Disagree	Strongly disagree
M	The head gathers the information necessary for making decisions	Strongly agree	Agree	Disagree	Strongly disagree
P	Staff feel able to disagree with the head in meetings	Strongly agree	Agree	Disagree	Strongly disagree

C	There are good systems for keeping people informed	Strongly agree	Agree	Disagree	Strongly disagree
V	The ethos of the school is effectively de-motivating	Strongly agree	Agree	Disagree	Strongly disagree
M	The head asks the question 'what if …'	Strongly agree	Agree	Disagree	Strongly disagree
E	The head directly confronts poor performance	Strongly agree	Agree	Disagree	Strongly disagree
D	Staff who have been appointed to new jobs are no longer treated as full members of the staff	Strongly agree	Agree	Disagree	Strongly disagree
S	People with difficulties do not ask for help	Strongly agree	Agree	Disagree	Strongly disagree
V	All staff are working with a shared purpose	Strongly agree	Agree	Disagree	Strongly disagree

Appendix 6.2

Interview Schedule

(1)   What opportunities are there for professional development of staff? Which staff?

Jobs-search, application, after appointment?

What effect does this have on staff morale – on children's learning?

(2)   How are staff kept informed of decisions and situations which affect them?

Formal/informal systems

Teaching/non-teaching staff

How effective?

How does it impact on children's learning and behaviour?

(3)   Do staff know what is expected of them in terms of tasks and professional conduct?

How do they know? How are the expectations expressed?

Are they high? Reasonable? Unreasonable?

How do they affect pupil learning and behaviour?

(4)   Can you describe the decision-making processes in this school?

Curriculum – other aspects

School development planning – policy making

Role of co-ordinator

Involvement – interviewee/others

Whose opinions sought?

Do people give opinions/disagree?

What effect does the way decisions are made have on their effectiveness in terms of children's learning and behaviour?

(5) How would you describe the leadership vision for this school?

Is it related to children's learning?

How is the vision applied? What steps are taken to achieve the vision?

Does it influence children's learning?

Forward planning? Information gathering?

How effective is it?

(6) If staff had any difficulties with any aspect of their job, who would they go to for help?

What support would they expect?

General: How do you think leadership behaviour affects the learning and development of children in the school?

References

Angus, L. (1989) "New leadership and the possibility of educational reform" in J. Smyth (ed.) *Critical Perspectives on Educational Leadership*. (Reprinted 1998) London: The Falmer Press.

Bhindi, N. and Duignan, P. (1997) "Leadership for a new century: authenticity, intentionality, spirituality and sensibility", *Education Management and Administration*, 25, (2), 117-32.

Bush, T. and Middlewood, D. (eds.) (1997) *Managing People in Education*. London: Paul Chapman.

Dimmock, C. and O'Donoghue, T.A. (1997) *Innovative School Principals and Restructuring; Life History Portraits of Successful Managers of Change*. London: Routledge.

Drucker, P.F. (1979) *Management*. London: Pan Books.

Evers, C.W. (1992) "Ethics and ethical theory in educative leadership: a pragmatic and holistic approach" in P.A. Duignan and R.J.S. MacPherson (eds.) *Educative Leadership: A Practical Theory for New Administrators and Managers*. London: Falmer Press.

Foster, W. (1989) "Toward a critical practice of leadership" in J. Smyth (ed.) *Critical Perspectives on Educational Leadership*. (Reprinted 1998) London: Falmer Press.

Fullan, M. and Hargreaves, A. (1992) *What's Worth Fighting For in Your School? Working Together for Improvement*. Milton Keynes: Open University Press.

Grace, G. (1995) *School Leadership: Beyond Education Management. An Essay in Policy Scholarship*. London: Falmer Press.

Hall, V. and Southworth, G. (1997) "Headship", *School Leadership and Management*, 17, (2), 151-70.

Hallinger, P., Murphy, J. and Hausmann, C. (1993) "Conceptualizing school restructuring: principals' and teachers' perceptions" in C. Dimmock (ed.) *School Based Management and School Effectiveness*. London: Routledge.

Marks, H.M. and Louis, K.S. (1997) "Does teacher empowerment affect the classroom? The implications of teacher empowerment for instructional practice and student academic performance", *Educational Evaluation and Policy Analysis*, 19, (3), 245-75.

Northfield, J. (1992) "Leadership to promote quality in learning" in P.A. Duignan and R.J.S. MacPherson (eds.), *Educative Leadership: a Practical Theory for New Administrators and Managers*. London: Falmer Press.

Spaulding, A. (1997) "Life in schools – a qualitative study of teacher perspectives on the politics of principals: ineffective leadership behaviours and their consequences upon teacher thinking and behaviour", *School Leadership and Management*, 17, (1), 39-55.

Chapter Seven

The Role of the Deputy Headteacher in Managing Change

DESPITE recent research (Hughes and James, 1999; Southworth, 1997; Ribbins, 1997), the role of deputy headship continues to be overlooked by policy planners who seem more eager to make their mark on the educational landscape at the beginning of a teacher's career, qualified teacher status (QTS) induction or through the devising of more targets and threshold stages needed to become an advanced skills teacher (AST). As a result the deputy's role has often been overshadowed yet, increasingly, as this chapter outlines, he or she is often the one responsible for managing major initiatives. Mandy Goggin, an experienced deputy head-teacher of a church primary school, whose career has spanned several posts together with experience outside education, undertook the 'Preparation for Leadership' course, an eight session programme that aims to provide skills training in management issues for co-ordinators and aspiring deputies. She has been instrumental as a change agent both from the perspective of deputy and through a sustained period of acting headship.

The Study

The 1988 Education Reform Act initiated a massive cultural change as well as aiding greater managerialism for primary schools. This continued with the publication of a report by the DES (1990) which outlined the need for headteachers to be provided with appropriate training and development.

However, it was not until the introduction of the national professional qualification for headship in 1996 that two important questions were raised. First, what is the most effective way of developing and managing an appropriate headship curriculum, and secondly, what provision is made for career deputies, unwilling or unable to enrol on the NPQH course, yet nevertheless encharged with similar challenges to manage change in their own school?

Goggin argued that all the interviewees in her sample, and more from her experience, fulfilled the role of director of curricular studies identified by Harrison and Gill (1992: 53) as curriculum leader responsible for co-ordinators, pupil assessment, record keeping and whole school curriculum review. Although the national professional qualifications modules are not specifically concerned with management of change theories, implementation, acceptance, resistance and self-renewal, there remain aspects of strategic direction and development, leading and managing staff that nevertheless address such issues in a depth that non-participants could only gain through award-bearing management courses or a programme of highly structured guided reading. As such, this study is illuminating in recording some of the approaches of deputy headteachers in their role as change managers. Their interpretation of this, together with their formal responsibilities, is a useful starting point, particularly as the DfEE (1998) document on teachers' pay remains somewhat vague about their professional duties.

> A person appointed deputy headteacher in a school, in addition to carrying out the professional duties of a teacher other than a head-teacher ... shall play a major role under the overall direction of the headteacher in:
>
> (a) formulating the aims and objectives of the school;
> (b) establishing the policies through which they shall be achieved;
> (c) managing staff and resources to that end; and
> (d) monitoring progress towards their achievement.

The Sample

As a deputy headteacher, Goggin had experienced overload, completing her MA, undertaking a module in the national professional qualifications course as well as acting as literacy co-ordinator in school. All this had followed a period of acting headship during an interregnum. Questioned about this she agreed that this was a punishing workload and had possibly used the research to try and establish some measure of comparability. This led to a follow-up enquiry about gathering a sample. Former colleagues and fellow course members returned favours and so tended to make up the bulk of any sample, and initially it was debatable as to how representative these people were. As Goggin agreed, the inevitability of skewing such a group towards the professionally enriched cannot be overlooked. However, the school backgrounds of rural, urban, junior, and grant maintained created more of a balance although admittedly the absence of men was a drawback. Just as Bell (1993) cautioned against bias in documentation but did not dismiss its value, so this sample still has much to offer as a basis for preliminary analysis.

Goggin interviewed seven deputy headteachers, all women aged between thirty and fifty, for between 35-40 minutes each. She decided to tape the interviews, not only to ensure accuracy, but also as a way to gauge tone of voice and possible hesitations which could prove illuminating. A pilot schedule was devised consisting of fourteen questions (see Appendix 7.2). Questions 1 and 2 about career routes and current responsibilities have been summarised in the table drawn up as Appendix 7.1. However, the following responses give an indication of deputy headteachers' responsibilities:

'I'm in charge of the curriculum totally – Mr X leaves it completely to me.' (Deputy D)

'I'm responsible for overall curriculum monitoring and development (with no non-contact time).' (Deputy B)

For most interviewees, the deputy headteachers' curriculum remained an integral part of their role as the above references illustrate. One respondent claimed 'she felt the need to drive the curriculum because otherwise nothing would happen in the school' and three of them had been responsible for introducing the national literacy strategy. However, looking at the table (see Appendix 7.1), most would appear to be just as involved in staff development issues as curriculum and change management. With the focus of the interview questions on change, it is interesting to consider responses to question 3 on recent curriculum changes. The positive responses to this question are perhaps surprising, with one deputy headteacher claiming that for as long as she had been in education there had always been change, a comment that perhaps reflects the new breed of post 1988 Education Reform Act professional who is coming through to management positions. This view was exemplified by Fullan's (1993: 3) view of the education system:

> On the one hand, we have the constant and ever expanding presence of educational innovation and reform ... On the other hand, however, we have an educational system which is fundamentally conservative.

This can be interpreted as conservative in its current approach to literacy and numeracy, booster classes and inspection. Yet, as one deputy headteacher (Cath) argued, because the changes were externally driven, 'schools are not developing the things which are pertinent to them' in terms of innovation and reform and so felt restricted. Just as important, staff reactions as reported by Cath and other respondents, were somewhat different, with words like 'threatened', 'frightened' and 'stressed' being used.

In answer to question 4 on change and the school development plan, not surprisingly, the value of school development planning was agreed by all, but the need to prepare people in the developing culture for change in the school was seen by two interviewees as particularly important. The danger of not consulting, rather than openness and widespread communication, was identified as a major flaw leading to resistance. Cath argued that 'really successful schools personalise the change – they take on board what they need to and don't lose sight of where they want to go'. This concurs with many of Buchanan and Boddy's (1992) characteristics of effective change agents. However, it must be borne in mind that these people as deputy headteachers are all part of the process while for those teachers described by Duck (1993: 109):

> Change is inescapably and intensely personal, because it requires people to do something different, to think something different and to feel something different.

Nonetheless, as Goggin recorded, some of the interviewees demonstrated an awareness of the problem-solving strategies to deal with change, something that could be explored further with future research.

Linked to question 4, the fifth question on staff involvement was an area that elicited little information from the respondents. The reasons for this, but not necessarily the blame, could be traced back to the leadership style of the headteacher. As Wallace and Huckman (1999: 2) commented:

> Primary heads have therefore become – comparatively recently – more dependent on their staff, and many are ... sharing the management burden through some form of team approach. In small schools, the entire professional staff may be conceived as a single team.

Nevertheless, Wallace and Huckman conceded that there was a downside to this, particularly if the team failed to perform effectively. In the eyes of any external assessor, for example OFSTED, the leadership of the headteacher will be called into question. In short, securing staff commitment to policy decisions is necessary (Bell and Rhodes, 1996), if not essential, and this can only be achieved through maximum involvement.

When questioned about their role in 'change' (question 6) Dawn recognised that she was at the forefront of any changes, overseeing everything through a participative approach of curriculum teamwork, with four members to plan, implement, evaluate and review. In doing this she appeared to be fulfilling the co-ordinating, inter-personal, quality assurance and strategic overview areas referred to by Garrett and McGeachie (1999) in their Sheffield study as issues respondents most frequently mentioned as important. Clearly the advantage of being non-classroom based cannot be under-estimated yet for others the commitment to learning remains strong either through internal staff programmes or drawing on outside specialists such as advisory teachers to reinforce the message. Despite their good intentions none of the deputy headteachers regularly carried out monitoring evaluation and review in classrooms. Financial constraints appeared to be the sole excuse; however, one can but wonder as to the culture of the school where the headteacher carries out such duties whilst leaving the deputy trapped in what Southworth (1997a: 24) termed 'the classroom cyberspace':

> They become virtual deputies trapped in the cyberspace of their own classrooms unable to influence directly what is happening around the school.

Once again the mechanisms for achieving non-contact time along with what Hughes and James (1999: 90) described as 'the deputy's willingness to conform and accept the head's style of management' would have provided another fruitful area for analysis. Nevertheless, all the deputy headteachers mentioned informal monitoring, looking at displays of work and examining planning, as part of their informal monitoring role. Goggin's possible explanation that schools are not developing the correct organisational culture is an interesting one supported by Morrison (1998: 177):

> An appropriate culture for change in the organisation emphasises openness synergy and widespread communication, building in and on feedback.

Yet earlier the impression given was one of team work and, for some, overall curriculum responsibility that should allow them opportunities to shape such important collaborative processes as monitoring and receiving feedback within a climate of improvement. Question 7 focused on the financial changes and the varying degrees of involvement. Setting aside the lack of practical experience, Goggin's point about financial planning and awareness is revealing. For at the simplest level these people are ignoring a key strand of what Leigh (1998: 14) described as the strategic rope, 'three woven-together strands, technical, cultural and political, that knit together to implement and help make change permanent'. Hence, despite their sporadic involvement in budget discussions and some attendance at governors' meetings, overall it would appear that deputy headteachers allowed a diminution of the role which in turn could only hinder them as change agents. Perhaps more emphasis is needed on what Wilson (1992: 106) referred to as the 'broker role' – creating and maintaining a power base, effective negotiation and influencing skills, effective oral presentation. All of these might provide them with scope to resource sufficient non-contact time for them to fulfil their other management duties adequately.

In general, financial responsibility, the subject of question 7, was an area respondents admitted they lacked expertise in, which parallels the findings of Garrett and McGeachie (1999). Most believed, however, that despite only a basic knowledge, if they became acting headteacher they would 'learn fast'. Clearly a lack of non-contact time is an issue but one which only partly explains the discrepancy, which raised the questions shown in Appendix 7.3 and which are discussed later in this chapter.

Replies to the question of staff responses to change provoked discussions which centred on resistance, pressure and stress. Overall, however, it was encouraging to find that despite some initial resistance most teachers remained fairly positive towards change although those who had been in the same school for more than ten years felt under the greatest pressure. Dalin *et al.* (1993: 12) referred to four main barriers to acceptance:

(1) Value barriers: where the proposed change challenges one's values system or if one does not agree with the proposed values.

(2) Power barriers: where people may accept the change if it brings them greater power, conversely they may resist it if it reduces their power.

(3) Psychological barriers: where people resist the challenge to their security, confidence and emotional well being.

(4) Practical barriers: where people will resist change if it threatens to de-skill them, if the investment in re-skilling is too daunting or if the resources are insufficient to support the change.

One interviewee stressed the value of a supportive environment as a prerequisite for success. The staff perspective that 'they are all in this to-gether' and all 'share the vision for the school' is obviously a gratifying one. However, one deputy headteacher felt that certain problems over staff resist-ance would have been alleviated 'if there had been more forward planning' and time taken to sensitise staff.

When it came to responding to the question of the deputy head-teacher's role in the change process (question 9) Goggin acknowledged the overlap with question 6. However, it was interesting to record responses to her supplementary question about the extent to which staff had reviewed and evaluated the changes which had occurred. None of her sample had appeared to do so formally despite such a process being a key component of any change model.

Respondents in answer to question 10 on resource implications focused on the financial and material rather than the most important – human resources, as emphasised by Gilmore and Fraleigh (1993: 75):

> What must change is the way we manage the only unlimited resource we have ... the value-adding capacity of the workforce.

Gill, though, described her work with Friends of the School as part of a wider brief to liaise with parents and form a working party to improve the school environment, something that could be loosely interpreted as develop-ing human resources. These external links led to the final three questions concerned with external relationships and specifically contact with the governors.

Three of the respondents claimed they had provided governors with information about curriculum changes; others, however, mentioned the 'hands-off' role seemingly adopted by many. Enid's comment that governors who work in business 'find it difficult to relate to how education works' is a concerning one. The majority of the deputy headteachers believed that it should be part of their role to keep governors informed, not least, as part of their professional development. This highlights another important management area, as cited by Everard and Morris (1990), where briefings and papers should be kept jargon free and user friendly.

On the value of parental involvement, however, there appeared to be greater evidence of relationship building and information giving, although, once again it was largely curriculum weighted. The need 'to keep parents on your side' was important to a number of the respondents although they all recognised the benefits of greater external involvement.

Reflections and Further Thought on the Study

Some areas of the study seemed to be underdeveloped and consequently the authors designed a set of questions to investigate further these issues with Goggin (see Appendix 7.3 for actual questions). The first question was designed as an icebreaker to allow her to think back to the research sample and her data collection as discussed earlier in the chapter, and the rest to expand on the research.

Job Descriptions

In the study there was a lack of documentary evidence available, particularly regarding job descriptions as outlined in further details for applicants. In the past this has provided a rich source of comparative data, particularly when attempting to match the intentional with the actual and from there establishing specific zones of management responsibility. Although the research addressed this through questioning (see Appendix 7.1), Goggin admitted some regret in not pursuing it more formally. When such documentation is not offered there is a limit to how persistent one can be within the boundaries of research conventions. Johnson (1994) argued that interviewing, despite its focus and purpose, has to remain a social encounter for the goodwill to remain and in that sense the degree of probing is necessarily limited.

Notwithstanding such restrictions, Goggin agreed that all the deputy headteachers interviewed demonstrated a lack of strategic planning knowledge. For some there was an element of consultation rather than jointly sitting down together to plan and develop a vision, although all chose to stress the operational nature of their work.

Deputies' Awareness of Change

That same lack of awareness could be found in the responses to change where the researcher admitted that again she had probed insufficiently. Looking back at her questions in this area it is hard to defend answers that do not introduce a certain theoretical perspective, particularly given the academic background of the sample. One respondent had recently gained an MA in Education Management, another had a higher degree in education studies whilst two more were engaged in NPQH training. What did become apparent through questioning Goggin was the lack of knowledge and lack of in-service support in the area of change management. Goggin's view coincided with local authority advisers and inspectors when she claimed: 'Schools are good at implementing [change], reasonable at evaluating but not good at handling data or establishing specific success criteria.'

Such a criticism set against the background of general success in the literacy hour appears at first to be unwarranted. Upon closer examination, however, criticisms levied by David Reynolds (1999), adviser to the government on the numeracy hour strategy, do much to explain such failings:

> It is a problem if you lay things down from the centre, you create a profession which becomes accustomed to having things laid down for it. Now the worry is that as things change so rapidly that you may have a profession that is slightly disabled, which is why I think what one needs to do and I don't disagree with anything that has been done, I have supported this wholeheartedly, what one needs to do is to move beyond giving foundations to people and prescribing for persons to a situation whereby we skill people to make more decisions for themselves to actually react to a changing environment in creative ways.

Monitoring by Deputy Headteachers

This focused on the lack of monitoring by deputy headteachers, except for those two involved in the national professional qualifications for headship training. Once again it was hard to draw conclusions without a more detailed knowledge of the school organisation. Those who offered an excuse for their lack of monitoring invariably mentioned time constraints, although

Goggin attributed this more to leadership styles within a restricted learning culture. In short, the real reason may lie with the willingness of the head-teacher to make it happen or perhaps the unwillingness of the deputy to lay him or herself open to challenge and conflict in areas of parallel rather than superior competence.

Such a simplistic explanation only gains credence if one examines the generally high tolerance and levels of acceptance by staff recorded in this study and elsewhere (Smith and Sykes, 2000). Their one stability zone, according to Toffler (1971), lies in the classroom – their classroom – where unwilling consultants are admitted to advise on specifics and parents welcomed in a subordinate role. But the prospect of another teacher, whether co-ordinator or deputy headteacher regularly monitoring their work, is often a bridge too far particularly for those with ten years experience in that school (and often in the same classroom).

Budgeting Areas

In response to the question of budgeting areas, Goggin agreed that the implications of not getting involved (see Appendix 7.3) was a tricky area and a difficult one to assess based on interview alone. As she explained, it is only when you become acting headteacher that you realise how much is ultimately down to computer packages and what level of financial planning can be bought in. She believed that many interviewees felt time with the secretary was not well spent, and a few had tried to become more involved but there were often competing demands. Once again she agreed that the headteacher needed to give priority to management time for budgeting to make it work.

Coping with Change

On the issue of staff resistance and the implications for experienced teachers with more than ten years experience in one school, Goggin reiterated her belief in the importance of maintaining a team approach. She questioned, citing Huberman's (1988) model, how performance-related pay would equate with the need to maintain motivation amongst all staff members. In her interviews a number of deputy headteachers developed the theme of initial staff resistance, being 'quite phased by numeracy', whilst perhaps more worryingly one deputy referred to a 'talented and experienced staff member who is disillusioned and depressed'. For others, the fact that staff viewed change as something that 'they are all in together' as 'they all share the vision for the school' is heartening despite having implications for new pay structures when threshold payments run the risk of destroying collegiality.

Evaluation of Change Programmes and the Role of the Local Education Authority

Here a strongly held view was that headteachers needed to do more in promoting and being encouraged to promote the necessary cultural shift. As Goggin commented:

> Monitoring, evaluating and review (MER) is claimed to be taking place but schools need to consider what to do next, how they are keeping objectives in sight, maintaining their provision and not just ticking over.

Certainly this view confirms findings from other research conducted by Smith and Sykes (2000) carried out across a selected sample of twenty primary schools.

Deputies as Curriculum Managers

Deputy headteachers as curriculum managers, rather than school leaders, provoked a similar response that once again illustrates the value of national professional qualifications for headship training. As Goggin argued:

> Questions about where the school should be in five years time are crucial. If you are going to improve the quality of learning, you have got to have ideas about effective teaching and learning strategies. From there you can move to parents and governors. Some may think it is not their role but this is the path towards greater involvement. It is also a way to involve heads more.

Interestingly, this topic led to a discussion about the current division in continuing professional development between headteachers and deputies; with the somewhat cynical observation of one group going away to a luxury hotel for a leadership programme whilst another worked at home for a qualification. Goggin's belief that there should be considerably more emphasis on joint planning and development is difficult to counter.

Advisers Involved in Succession Planning

This was an idea floated by one of the deputy headteachers interviewed, and whose genesis in education could be traced to the DES (1990). Here Drucker's (1977: 312) view of managerial jobs seems particularly relevant:

> All managerial jobs should be designed to provide satisfaction through performance. The job should challenge and reward. If the main satisfaction of the job is promotion, the job itself has lost significance and meaning.

Perhaps more important, before even any pilot schemes for acceleration through the ranks are considered, those responsible might look no further again than to Drucker and his views on the subject.

> The worst thing a company can do is to try to develop the 'comers' and leave out the others. Ten years hence 80 per cent of the work will have to be done by those left out. If they have not developed themselves to the point where they can understand, accept, and put into action the vision of the few 'comers', nothing will happen. The eight out of every ten who were not included in the programme will, understandably, feel slighted. They may end up by becoming less effective, less productive, less willing to do new things than they were before.
>
> The attempt to find 'potential' is altogether futile. It is less likely to succeed than simply choosing every fifth person. Performance is what counts, and the correlation between promise and performance is not a particularly high one. Five out of every ten 'high potential' young workers turn out to be nothing but good talkers by the time they reach forty. Conversely, five out of every ten young employees who do not look 'brilliant' and do not talk a good game will have proven their capacity to perform by the time they are in their early forties.
>
> Also, the idea that the purpose of management development is to find 'replacements' negates the entire reason for the activity. We need management development precisely because tomorrow's jobs and to-morrow's organisations are going to be different from today's jobs and today's organisations. If all we had to do were to replace yesterday's and today's jobs, we would be training people as apprentices under their present bosses.
>
> The worst kind of replacement planning is the search for a 'crown

prince'. A crown prince either has a legal right to succeed, or else being chosen is likely to destroy him. No matter how carefully concealed, picking a crown prince is an act that the whole organisation very rapidly recognises. And then all the other possible contenders unite against the crown prince and work to bring him down – and they usually succeed. (330)

This brings us to Ribbin's (1999: 3) questions about a leadership curriculum for prospective headteachers under the auspices of the national professional qualifications for headship, that he put to the Chief Executive of the Teacher Training Agency when the initial programme was being outlined:

> What is good leadership? What is a good leader? How can those with good potential be identified and encouraged to prepare for leadership? How can those with significant leadership responsibilities be encouraged to improve? How good is the evidence? What should a curriculum for developing and sustaining good leaders and leadership look like? How should it be taught? What standards should it entail? How should it be assessed? How good is the evidence? What is the evidence that if such a curriculum were to be developed and taught, it would have significant beneficial effect on how those graduating actually lead?

Dalin and Rolff's (1993: 89) model offered one solution when it outlined the value profile of a school that places teacher support and mutual trust at the core, together with student learning.

Non-contact Time for Deputies

It was up to the headteacher, as Goggin said, to give real leadership and, by implication, create time. However, some latitude by the local education authority would appear essential. But as recent studies (Smith and Sykes, 2000; Southworth, 1997b) revealed, non-contact time remained the key issue in unlocking the future potential for innovation and improvement.

There is no doubt that the demands of deputy headship are considerable and like all teachers pressures increased enormously over the last years of the twentieth century. However, as a manager and assistant headteacher, the role in relation to change management and external relationships has also developed to the extent that the demands of the post require a great deal of support and training. Increased responsibilities as curriculum manager, change agent and external liaison require updating coupled with significant release time.

Recommendations

- A clarification of the title and increase in status to *stress* the assistant headteacher aspect
- A minimum of two days non-contact time for management training and curriculum monitoring
- Professional updating in areas such as human resource management, change and evaluation
- Greater involvement with the governing body and possible co-option where rules allow
- Rotation of management responsibilities with the headteacher in agreement with the chair of governors and the local education authority adviser.

Appendix 7.1

Summarised Career Routes

Interviewees	Years as Deputy Head	Type of School Number on role	Career Route
Beryl	3½	C Junior, 250	Mainstream + special A → B allowance Internal 2 terms acting headteacher
Cath	3	CE, 245	A + B allowances, small and large school experience, co-ord range wide experience of key stages
Dawn	4	CP large Two form entry	25 years teaching experience internal promotion

Enid	2 acting deputy head		7 years SENCO B allowance
Fay	2	CE One form entry	7 years KS1 B allowance
Gill	2 acting deputy head senior tutor	Methodist Junior	20 years in the school A → B allowance
Helen	1 term	Rural, 148	Broad KS experience

Summarised Current Responsibilities

Interviewees	Main responsibilities	NCT roles shared with Headteacher
Beryl	Literacy co-ordinator SD appraisal, INSET Overall curriculum Monitoring and development	
Cath	SD appraisal, INSET Maintain standards Discipline	
Dawn	NO co-ord responsibility but I/C curriculum Literacy co-ordinator SD appraisal, INSET	
Enid	Headteacher long-term sick Helped by associate head 2 days per week	
Fay	Literacy co-ordinator SD INSET Appraisal if not written down comes to me	Communication rather than curriculum feedback to headteacher
Gill	SD appraisal, INSET Partnership	
Helen	Y5/6 teachers Non labelled jobs, e.g. setting a good example	Operational

Appendix 7.2

Interview Questions

(1) Could you please tell me about your career so far?

(2) As deputy head, what are your main roles and responsibilities?

(3) There is currently a great deal of curriculum change taking place with literacy, numeracy, assessment and Curriculum 2000, school home contracts, LMS etc. What are your views on this?

(4) Do you feel that change is currently being managed via the school development plan?

(5) (a) If yes – how are you involved in this process?
     (b) If no – how could change be managed more effectively?

(6) What is your role in this change (training, implementation, MER etc)?

(7) Are you involved in the financial changes taking place in school (LMS and the increasing practice of buying in services)?

(8) How do you feel staff are coping with these changes in primary education?

(9) Has your role as deputy head involved leading and managing them through this process? How have you done this?

(10) Such changes may have had resourcing implications (staffing, books etc). How have you been involved?

(11) Have/are the governors aware of the current and future changes?

(12) Do you feel that you as deputy head should encourage them to become involved?

(13) Have you been involved in providing parents with information about the changes? Did you feel that this was a useful exercise?

(14) Finally, thank you for your time and have you anything further you would wish to add?

Appendix 7.3

MA – The Role of the Primary Deputy in the Management of Change

(1) What promoted this area of interest? How did you set about gathering a sample? How representative were they?

(2) In the answers on roles and responsibilities did you see evidence of job descriptions? How much difference was there? The impression given was of a lack of strategic planning in the role. To what extent was this the case?

(3) Regarding change, many deputies appeared a little vague in this area. What was your perception? What reasons/explanations can you offer?

(4) There appeared a general lack of monitoring by deputies. However, Cath, as an NPQH candidate, was more involved. How many others were enrolled on the programme and what should be the procedure for other deputies?

(5) The same seems to apply in budgeting areas. Is there a message here or are deputies using finance and lack of contact time as an excuse, e.g. more involvement, more status, more NCT, less involvement, less status, classroom-based, eventually the post diminishes and finally disappears?

(6) Coping with change appears to be an issue for teachers more than ten years in post. Are there positive messages in the Green Paper here?

(7) Lack of evaluation of change programmes appeared a weakness. Any recommendations to address this? What is the role of the LEA?

(8) The impression remains of deputies still being curriculum managers rather than whole school leaders. How can schools improve in this area?

(9) You suggest that advisers should be involved in succession planning. What kind of programme do you envisage? Are there potential pitfalls here, particularly given the number of church schools in the north west of England?

(10) To provide deputies with 0.2 non-contact time in 500 primaries would cost 500 x £120 x 40, approximately £2.4 million, and give them parity with NQTs. Is this feasible, and how can resources be found?

References

Bell, L. and Rhodes, C. (1996) *The Skills of Primary Management*. London: Routledge.

Bell, J. (1993) *Doing Your Research Project* (2nd edn). Milton Keynes: Open University Press.

Buchanan, D. and Boddy, D. (1992) *The Expertise of the Change Agent*. London: Prentice Hall.

Dalin, P., Rolff, H. and Kottkamp, R. (1993) *Changing the School Culture*. London: Cassell.

DES (1990) *School Management Task Force Report*. London: DES Publications.

DfEE (1998) *School Teacher's Pay and Conditions Document*. London: DfEE Publications.

Drucker, P.F. (1979) *Management*. London: Pan Books.

Duck, J. (1993) "Managing change: the art of balancing", *Harvard Business Review*, Nov/Dec, 109-18.

Everard, B. and Morris, G. (1990) *Effective School Management*. London: Paul Chapman.

Fullan, M. (1993) *Change Forces: Probing the Depth of Educational Reform*. London: Falmer Press.

Garrett, V. and McGeachie, B. (1999) "The role of the deputy head in the primary school", *School Leadership and Management*, 19, (1), 67-81.

Gilmore, S.K. and Fraleigh, P.W. (1993) *Communication at Work*. Oregon: Friendly Press.

Harrison, M. and Gill, S. (1992) *Primary School Management*. London: Heinemann Educational Publications.

Huberman, M. (1988) "Teacher careers and school improvement", *Journal of Curriculum Studies*, 20, (2), 119-32.

Hughes, M. and James, C. (1999) "The relationship between the head and deputy head in primary schools", *School Leadership and Management*, 19, (1), 83-95.

Johnson, D. (1994) *Research Methods in Educational Management*. Harlow: Longman.

Leigh, A. (1994) *Effective Change*. London: IPM Publications.

Morrison, K. (1998) *Management Theories for Successful Change*. London: Paul Chapman.

Reynolds, D. "Interview" in *Analysis*, BBC Radio 4, 1999 November.

Ribbins, P. (1999) "Educational administration and the Search for Sophia". Paper presented at BEMAS Conference, Manchester: UMIST.

Southworth, G. (1997a) "The deputy dilemma", *Managing Schools Today*, 6, (9), 24-5.

Southworth, G. (1997b) *Inside Deputy Headship*. Berkshire: University of Reading.

Toffler, A. (1971) *Future Shock*. London: Pan Books.

Wallace, M. and Huckman, L. (1999) *Senior Management Teams in Primary Schools: The Quest for Synergy*. London: Routledge.

Wilson, D.C. (1992) *A Strategy of Change*. London: Routledge.

Chapter Eight

Marketing Strategies and their Influence in the Primary School

MORE than a decade after the 1988 Education Reform Act and the introduction of local management of schools, it is interesting to observe how schools have responded to the 'quasi-market' referred to by Woods (1994). He described how the reforms that enhanced parental choice were to act as a lever of change in schools which as a consequence would deliver a consumer-driven product. He pointed out the paradox that schools have had their product dictated in many important areas by central government. The National Curriculum, for example, limits curriculum variety across the nation's schools. In the late 1990s the context in which schools operated underwent further change with the publication of league tables and other performance indicators. Parents of all social groups are becoming increasingly aware of the criteria by which schools are judged and, therefore, exercise their right to a choice within the educational market. With resource allocation linked to the size of the pupil roll, primary school managers need to think very carefully about the relationship between their school and the local community as their existence may rely on nothing less than their popularity with their neighbours.

Gordon Core, the deputy headteacher of a primary school in an area with surplus school places as a result of a changing population profile, became interested in the use of marketing strategies in primary schools and headteachers' attitudes to such practices. Schools under the threat of closure had, in his experience, involved local celebrities, councillors and members of parliament. He was interested to discover to what extent schools view their activities as marketing, how widespread marketing activities are and what value headteachers place on such practices. This investigation was undertaken as part of his MA in Education Management.

The Study

Core's interest was not restricted to marketing activities in schools where competition for pupil numbers is most acute, as it was in the schools in his immediate locality. For this reason the eleven headteachers were carefully selected to reflect diversity in terms of experience in post and the different group and classification of their school, spread across four local education authorities. Interest was also focused on the role of the local authorities in marketing their schools.

A personal view of the purpose and power of marketing in primary schools was expressed throughout the study, for Core believed that it provided an opportunity to view the school through the eyes of the customer and the consumer, to identify areas of match and mismatch between the school's intentions and perceived action and, most importantly, to pinpoint effective ways of improving the service that the school offered. Throughout this survey the major client/customer was taken to be the parent. This can be shown to be the case in law from the 1944 Education Act onwards, although there has been much debate about the extent to which there is a clear cut customer/provider relationship in education, where a partnership between home and school is advocated. In addition to listening to the needs of the customer parents, and their consumer children, the task of school marketing is to provide hard information in an appropriate style that will enable them to see how the school can fulfil their education needs. Referring to Warner (1994), Core argued that the reputation of a primary school is built on the quality of reliability and trust in relationships. He also pointed out that marketing is not an aim in itself but consists of a series of goals to help the school achieve its aims. The objective of all marketing strategy is to influence the behaviour of the target audience. Ultimately, he believed marketing to be a tool for motivating the staff of a school, stimulating and challenging children's enthusiasms and tapping into vast sources of parental support for children's learning. Thus, marketing activities are placed at the heart of school improvement, inextricably linked to strategic planning and cannot be regarded as an optional extra.

Traditionally marketing has been viewed with suspicion by the not-for-profit public services, schools in particular. Commerce and industry have found it worthwhile to invest much effort, time, and money into marketing activities. This research was concerned with the possibility of schools learning valuable lessons about communication and organisation, subsequently translating them for use within a specific context.

A distinction was drawn between marketing which has sometimes been perceived as a hard-edged activity with aggressive and predatory overtones, deemed unsuitable for the primary school, and image promotion which may be seen as a softer approach, a passive, co-operative operation. It is possible to see these as two ends of a continuum, with schools' values and circumstances dictating their position on it, or to see image promotion as part of a marketing strategy.

The research contemplated a collection of headteachers' overall attitudes toward:

- marketing and its impact on their schools;
- their viewpoints on the necessity of marketing in the primary sector as a means of competing with neighbouring schools;
- the possible consequent effect on inter-school relations;
- identifying the needs of children and parents;
- their thoughts on the role of the local education authority within the marketing sphere;
- their customer care methods;
- how their school is portrayed within the local community.

The Sample

The sample comprised three female and eight male headteachers. Their experience of headship varied from between one term to fifteen years. There was a mix of suburban and rural schools with rolls from 68 to 452 pupils. Maintained local education authority, Church of England, Roman Catholic, and grant maintained schools were all represented. Some had inspections in the near future, one was facing possible closure and one was being rebuilt. Ten of the schools were from one of four local education authorities in the north west of England, the school that was grant maintained at the time of the research being in the same geographical region.

Core set out to find evidence of headteachers' attitudes and practice in relation to marketing. Therefore a qualitative approach was adopted and the research was conducted using tape-recorded, semi-structured interviews. This allowed the researcher the opportunity to cover the areas of relevance to the study whilst being able to gather richer data through face-to-face contact with fellow headteachers, which a questionnaire would not. A suitably piloted interview schedule contained questions about promotion of the school, the school brochure, attracting new intake pupils, the role of the local education authority and methods of obtaining feedback. Initial questions provided background information about the interviewees and their schools. As a result of two separate pilots the wording and subsequently the order of questions was changed to improve the flow of the interviews. The final schedule has been reproduced in Figure 8.1 below.

(1) What are the most important ways in which the school promotes a positive image within the local community?

(2) In what ways do you think that schools have changed in promoting their achievements over the last five years?

(3) What are the special factors in primary school marketing as opposed to marketing in industry?

(4) How important is the school brochure?

(5) Who is involved in the production of the school brochure?

(6) What other information, if any, do you provide for prospective parents; and how is it circulated throughout other agencies?

(7) What approaches do nearby schools employ in attracting pupils to their schools?

(8) What role does the LEA take in the promotion of your school and others in the local area?

(9) What strategies do you employ to ensure that help with marketing is obtained?

(10) What steps do you take to ensure you maximise your intake each September?

(11) How does your school obtain feedback from parents, and others, about its performance and image?

(12) Is there anything you would like to add about the marketing of your school?

Figure 8.1:   Final interview schedule

Results and Analysis

The evidence the respondents provided is suggestive of a wider picture but it is not possible to generalise too far as the sample could not be guaranteed to be fully representative of headteachers' views, even within the stated region.

Positive Image

The respondents were unanimous in their claims to be involved in active positive promotion of their schools in the local community. They aimed to provide

> approaches which promote the school as welcoming, both as a community and as a set of buildings; which foster problem-solving within a context which is understood by the parents; which offer involvement, and which demonstrate a willingness to listen ... (Glover *et al.*, 1996: 37).

All the headteachers advocated an open-door policy and stressed the importance of dealing with problems presented by parents. Only one respondent, however, saw this as a significant element in promoting a school's positive image. Each highlighted different areas but seven clearly believed community involvement was an important issue, and that it was a two-way process. Children were encouraged to participate in community events such as competitions and festivals while the community was invited to the school for summer fairs, open days and other activities. One headteacher, whose school was used as a polling station, exploited this as an opportunity to promote the school to adults who had limited access to school life. This type of activity adheres to Warner's (1994: 8) recommendation of positioning the school as an 'innovative and flexible institution within the community'. Harrison and Gill (1992) stressed the importance for schools to spread good news about their everyday creative and successful achievements. Four respondents were conscious of the significant contribution made by the local press. In some schools displays of press cuttings were on prominent display. One headteacher, in an area of falling rolls, directly attributed his increasing roll, drawn from a wider geographical area, to extensive press coverage.

In an area with a high proportion of denominational schools, the findings from affiliated schools were interesting. Church schools nurtured their relationship to their respective churches in order to project their image in the locality where tradition and word of mouth recommendations carried significance, especially where populations had remained static over a number of generations. One church school headteacher was able to attract large numbers of children from within the parish boundary and had seen a 33 per cent rise in the roll. Only one of the church schools had witnessed a slight decrease in school numbers as opposed to the majority of non-denominational schools in this small sample.

Despite claims for close community links, only four of the schools had any community use of their buildings and facilities out of school hours. Where such activities took place they included pre-school and after school care groups, children's uniformed organisations, a karate club and bingo evenings. One school had a building designed purely for community use and this was used extensively, not only throughout the school day, but also during the evenings and school holidays. A local youth organisation used another school during the holidays.

Of the eight schools that actively encouraged children to wear uniform, four interviewees believed it to be a key issue for school promotion. Children's behaviour in the locality was a reflection on their school standards. (Although not commented on it may have been the same belief that prevented some schools encouraging the wearing of a uniform.)

Promoting Achievements

All headteachers acknowledged that there had been significant changes in the way schools had publicised their achievements in the last five years. This was attributed to the greater availability of public information and the introduction of SAT testing with published league tables. Gorard's (1999: 32) research on school choice cited such information as having a considerable effect upon parents and their choice of school:

> To some extent, in an era when league tables of results are used as school performance indicators, and these results are generally presented in raw form, a desirable school is presented as one with high ability pupils.

Various reactions emerged, from one headteacher claiming the league tables had created 'a more competitive edge', to another seeing 'a worrying trend of competition' and a third viewing them as 'divisive'. Headteachers believed some schools were more aggressive than others in the promotion of such achievements. The interviewee in the grant maintained school commented that 'schools are now focused on performance to ensure that their standards are as good as the other schools in the neighbourhood'.

Those schools with least to fear tended to view the tables more positively.

The second major strand of change was more frequent use of media channels to promote achievements. These included newspaper reports and photographs, video recordings for other schools throughout their local education authority and radio broadcasts. Headteachers were eager to celebrate other aspects of school life in addition to academic achievements, including sport, music and educational visits.

Headteachers considered both strands of promotion as being influential with prospective parents. Other studies, (Smedley, 1995; Glover *et al.*, 1996), found that parents tended, when choosing schools, to rate academic results lower than certain other factors such as proximity to home and facilities. The views expressed by the headteachers suggested that schools themselves were now giving more weight to their academic reputation and a shift in parental perceptions since previous studies. By promoting all types of achievement schools put themselves forward as lively communities where teachers were willing to be involved in and beyond the basic curriculum. As child happiness is an important factor in school choice this type of promotion is useful. It also promotes the work of pupils and teachers and therefore enhances morale.

Primary School and Industrial Marketing

The reforms of both Conservative and Labour governments in Britain during the 1980s and 1990s followed a belief that markets and private sector management techniques could provide answers to the perceived deficiencies of the public sector and that if applied would result in improvements in standards of provision. A number of writers, including Keep (1992), advised caution in under-estimating the differences between private and public sectors. A state school operates with restrictions in the areas of revenue generation and budgetary control. For example, they cannot refuse to provide a service for those who incur disproportionate costs.

Nine of the headteachers acknowledged substantial differences. They usually referred to a major difference in the product. Education was primarily a people-centred activity, not perceived in terms of a commodity, as there was nothing tangible to advertise or sell. Two respondents recognised that a primary school had a restricted market. Accommodating a finite number of children, it could not usually expand and the local population could only offer a certain number of children to fill those places. It was also observed that there was a difference in the structure and specialisation in industry. 'A marketing manager could not concentrate on marketing whilst teaching all day and be a co-ordinator of umpteen subjects.' This comment reveals the widely felt professional belief that marketing is a distraction from the real business of education within the classroom, an optional extra.

Opinion ranged through a spectrum of understanding how lessons from the public sector could be applied to a tendency to reject them. One respondent thought industry was cold and calculating, and could afford to be as it retained more control of its product. Interestingly it was the child who was seen to embody 'unknown factors' rather than a centrally imposed curriculum limiting freedom to alter what was on offer. Another headteacher, however, expressed the view that:

> 'Any vision for the school involves a certain amount of expenditure ... we need children on seats to give you the money to do what you want to do with these children: so marketing matters.'

All the schools placed great emphasis on being caring organisations. Writers including Smedley (1995) confirmed the importance for school choice of perceived child happiness. Satisfying this parent need could be seen, Kotler and Armstrong (1996: 5) suggested, as marketing '... not in the old sense of making a sale ... but in the new sense of satisfying customer needs'.

The School Brochure

Every school is required by law to produce a brochure with statutory information. The sampled brochures revealed a lack of standardisation in structure and content. This could be deemed disadvantageous as it denied access to a format that would enable parents and children to make direct comparisons between schools. However, this same lack of standardisation allowed each primary school the opportunity to exploit its strengths within the clearly defined national framework.

The significance of the brochure uncovered a contrast in convictions. Eight headteachers valued the brochure. In one local education authority there was unanimous support for its importance. Some headteachers were conscious of the fact that it provided the first contact with many parents and they saw it as a tool, not only for giving information but also in selling the school. Warner (1994: 113) referred to the brochure as having potential to be used both as a reference and as guide for parents. This view was fully endorsed by a number of respondents.

Presentation was an important factor for at least half of the respond-ents, particularly the quality of print, with local printers being employed where in-house facilities were deemed not sufficiently professional. Appear-ance was not the only concern; content was equally valued. As one head-teacher put it: 'The brochure is a quality document of quality information.' One school used the services of a marketing agency at all stages of product-ion and distribution.

Two interviewees were not enthusiastic about the benefits of the school brochure. They saw it as an accepted document that was not particularly significant in the life of their schools. In both cases the schools were over-subscribed. Disappointment was expressed by one headteacher, about the level of parental feedback following dissemination of the brochure. Another placed more confidence on word-of-mouth communication in an area with low parental literacy. These examples highlight the importance of schools' identification of the wants and needs of the target market.

The headteachers involved were not concerned with financing the brochure; significantly only one respondent raised the issue of a possible capital waste.

All headteachers played a significant role in the creation of the brochure and all reported a team approach. The degree of involvement varied, with only four employing a whole school approach involving all teaching and non-teaching staff, governors, parents and children. Seven had active governor support. Headington and Howson (1995: 94) found wide in-volvement led to better understanding of the target market. Without it there was a danger of brochures merely being, 'statements of intent which demon-strated the expertise and control of the educationalist but were often bereft of the clients' wants and needs'.

Identifying Customer Needs

Market analysis is a method of gaining an understanding of the needs and expectations of the community. All headteachers thought that they had good relationships with their parents and that their schools were responding to parental wishes. Their responsiveness had not led to many changes in the school, since most felt that the type of education they provided was the result of the school's own planning; and that parents were happy with it.

They seemed to rely heavily on their open-door policies, parents' evenings and parent-teacher association (PTA) meetings as ways of receiving information about the image and performance of the school. This unsystematic approach, relying heavily on the parents volunteering incidental information on occasions with specific and different purposes, seems to imply that headteachers are not concerned with sampling regularly parental opinion on a wide range of school issues. Four schools had received useful feedback as a result of the recent innovation of home school agreements, whilst two others had learned more about parental expectations through parents meetings arranged to disseminate information on the government's literacy and numeracy strategies. Questionnaires to the whole parent population were issued at the time of inspection by all the schools and headteachers had noted comments made in inspectorate feedback. These examples show how schools can make use of data from a range of sources. However, the four initiatives above are part of national policy and do not represent an attempt by the school to seek information actively. Only five schools used their own questionnaires to analyse customer attitudes, needs and wants. Gorard (1999) found that parents appreciated programmes of choice. Three schools in the sample were disappointed in parental response. Parental apathy was also evident in schools' governors' annual report to parent meetings. Four respondents commented on low attendance.

In education, performing a needs assessment fulfils many of the requirements of a market analysis. However, a needs assessment must move beyond gathering information and into the complexities of problem-solving and priority setting. Only two headteachers employed a biannual cycle of questionnaires with the intention of creating a climate of continuous improvement whereby the information is fed into the school development planning process. In each of these schools governors were involved in marketing activities.

Sampling pupil and staff opinion was not asked about in this survey. Core acknowledged the role of internal marketing, quoting from Harrison and Gill (1992: 119):

> An internal audit will seek to assess the strengths and weaknesses of the school itself and the opportunities offered by its environment.

LEA Influence in the Marketing of Primary Schools

Gerwirtz *et al.* (1995) referred to the continuing significance of the role of the local education authority in the constitution of local education markets. According to the results of this survey, of limited scale, their involvement stopped short of marketing individual primary schools but use was made of combined statistics to promote education across the whole local authority. As one respondent put it 'the LEA is keen to say we have good schools'.

Five headteachers indicated that the local education authority had played a minor part in the promotion of their schools. This was in the form of offers for printing brochures and providing admission guidelines, and using their press office for press releases. In one case a school was asked to put on a display of work for a national literacy conference. The headteacher felt that the school was being promoted through this.

None of the respondents was aware of a local education authority marketing policy, nor had any consulted them on promoting their schools. Three headteachers from different authorities indicated that the authority had no involvement in marketing their schools. Local education authorities, according to Gewirtz et al. (1995), seem to operate as corporations rather than small businesses, trying to maximise the use of their school-place provision and minimise recoupment costs. This implies a franchise-type relationship between the authority and individual primary schools, imposing a limitation on the operation of the market, a tendency that target-setting may increase. One headteacher stated that the local education authority's marketing had a detrimental effect on the school and the local community because, 'it is trying to put forward an option of shutting us down'.

Schools and education authorities in a market model need to know what parents are looking for so that they can introduce policies to provide it and so ensure their own survival as well as increase customer satisfaction. According to Core, evidence suggested that the local education authorities lacked understanding of the importance of marketing in the primary sector. It may be that marketing individual schools is not an appropriate activity or a priority for these bodies. The research does indicate that the authorities and school strategy can be in conflict and that where this is the case the local education authority's interventions are likely to be perceived as unhelpful.

Marketing Strategies

The responses from the interviews revealed that there were no formal marketing strategies in place although there were varying degrees of marketing activity. Devlin and Knight (1990: 5) observed that, 'schools have always dealt with public relations, but often in an unsystematic, reactive and amateur way'. There were no committees. Only two schools had discussed marketing at governor level and only one had marketing incorporated in school development planning. In three schools promotion and marketing activities were exclusively driven by the headteacher. This singular approach was noted in research conducted by Kotler and Andreasen (1987), and by Devlin and Knight who noted:

> It's the headteacher's job to promote the school and make sure it's full or highly regarded in the community. It's not our job and we are not going to have anything to do with that side of the operation.

Three schools had adopted a stronger approach to marketing as a re-action to falling rolls. They viewed marketing activities as a way to attract pupil numbers. Each had a member of staff with responsibility to explore potential in this area. Interestingly none of these appointments was made up from members of staff with class responsibilities: they were, a bursar, a secretary acting as a public relations officer and a headteacher. One of these schools had engaged the services of a marketing agency and another had a member of staff attending a marketing course who stated that 'staying there is harder than getting there, but it is much harder to manage a shrinking school than a growing school'. These schools did not refer to marketing strategy but came the closest to describing a strategy without necessarily making the connection. Significantly, the three schools that acknowledged they were over-subscribed, did not recognise a need for a marketing strategy. One of these headteachers had subscribed to a school consortium that advised on marketing issues. He felt the feedback was of no great benefit to his school and subsequently withdrew from it.

Despite evidence of schools trying to maximise their intakes, a view co-existed that school enrolment is beyond the control of the individual school. The interviewees, on the whole, were willing to act as if a market existed but the conditions did not exist to reward their efforts. One respondent acknow-ledged that the measurement of an effective response to marketing was very difficult.

All the schools in the sample were active in the induction of new-intake children once on roll. Meetings took place in the summer term, prior to the new school year. Three schools had changed the format from a lecture style information-giving session, to more informal group sessions led by teachers. It was believed that this was more comfortable for the parents and so led to better communication. As Headington and Howson (1996: 94) reminded us: 'Educationalists often forget how traumatic a visit to school can be for non-professional parents.' Other activities included inviting pre-school children to assemblies and classroom visits, where opportunities for informal play or assessment tasks were offered; links with play-groups and nurseries; provision of child friendly 'brochures' and other paper communication. Parents were visited at home by staff from one school. Where recruitment is not an issue, customer satisfaction and the experience of the consumer are the logical *foci* of marketing activities. If marketing is not understood as an integral part of the educational provision of a school, such activities may not be appreciated as contributing to school promotion.

Market Competition

Interviewees were asked about the effects of marketing on their relations with neighbouring schools in an attempt to judge how the creation of a market might be affecting co-operation. Most of the schools did not feel they were in competition with other schools, nor did they wish to be. Keep (1992: 45) described the reluctance of schools to embrace profit sector marketing and remarked that schools attempted to avoid direct competition with one another. Five respondents indicated that they worked closely with their cluster schools. As one headteacher, who worked co-operatively within a cluster on September intakes commented: 'we do want to work alongside each other for the benefit of the local community, not in opposition to each other.' There was no evidence of competitor schools reinforcing negative messages during discussions with parents, although five headteachers were aware of such practices in other parts of their education authorities. Three headteachers felt that they were in competition with schools nearby. One believed that parental choice was the important factor and saw it as all-out competition; the other two did not. He felt that the competition for pupils amounted only to a little surreptitious poaching, whereas the others reported a feeling of competition resulting from anxiety about future league tables.

All this indicates that nurturing good relationships with existing customers is valued above aggressively competing with other schools. This ethos is at the heart of marketing within the non-profit service industries, implying the need for an introduction of a continuous system of monitoring which feeds into the development plan. This link has yet to be made in many primary schools.

Reflections on the Study

Core set out to investigate the current understanding of marketing as a management strategy in primary schools, and to examine the extent of marketing activities within the school and the value headteachers placed on marketing as a tool for school improvement.

He identified five areas for development that would lead to greater effectiveness. There was a need to

- implement formal marketing;
- identify customer needs;
- improve promotional literature;
- develop links with marketing agencies and embrace their expertise;
- take, where the local education authority was concerned, a more directive approach.

There is evidence of continued resistance to marketing. This is based on assumptions about the nature of marketing both in the private and public sector organisations. There remains a belief for some headteachers that a caring organisation is somehow incompatible with a marketing strategy and that its inherent goodness does not need to be actively promoted.

This misunderstanding allows many educationally congruent aspects of marketing and promotion to be in place but not recognised as marketing activities. They are seen as separate initiatives with an educational purpose, such as the programmes to induct children into the reception class.

Numerous marketing activities were uncovered during the research but little coherent planning. Indeed some headteachers, as a result of the interviews, reported having gained a wider view of marketing and expressed the intention of reviewing marketing within their schools to move towards a more integrated approach. The headteachers in the survey valued good relationships with parents and commitment from them, their staff and the pupils. What seemed to be missing was an appreciation of how marketing strategy could strengthen these, enhancing decision-making and leading to school improvement.

The employment of a formal marketing strategy may have the effect of increasing pupil numbers where that is an issue. Core, however, regarded this as almost a side issue. The benefit would be an organisation that became more effective as a result of listening and responding to feedback from every transaction connected with the school. He advocated that everyone had a part to play and that a team approach was needed because a school is a corporate entity that must be promoted as a body. In order to inaugurate and co-ordinate strategies he suggested that each school should have a designated senior member of staff with responsibility for marketing as well as a sub-committee of governors. Staff development is a crucial ingredient in development of school-wide skills and understanding.

Headteachers in oversubscribed schools expressed less interest in marketing. This may be part of the view that marketing is always about competition. Possibly these schools were active in promoting their achievements and that was one reason why they remained popular. Nevertheless it is clear that a perceived threat does sharpen schools' awareness of what constitutes marketing, leading to wider school involvement and, in some cases, the beginning of a strategic approach.

In general, a weak area of marketing strategy was the identification of customer needs. Existing data was not systematically scrutinised and few opportunities were created to sample parent opinion directly. Brochures and other contacts with home tended to be exclusively communication of the information-giving variety. There was little evidence of parental views influencing school policy; rather a belief that what was on offer was acceptable unless schools came to believe otherwise. This prevented schools becoming more customer-focused organisations. A tension existed between notions of professional expertise and control, and the recognition that greater responsiveness may be needed to ensure customer satisfaction.

It is significant that this aspect was lacking even in schools that as a result of falling rolls had begun to look more carefully at their attractiveness to potential parents. Time and money may be spent in the production of the brochure, but matching it to the wants and needs of the whole market is an essential element of effective communication.

Core believed that primary schools should consider the option of conferring with outside consultants on matters such as market research, public relations, advertising and brochure production, provided they already had a clear idea of their requirements. This may become an even more useful source of advice if local education authorities do not extend their involvement in marketing their schools and offering support to them. He saw no reason to reject the majority of marketing tools developed primarily for the private sector. He found the component parts of a strategy in many schools and agreed with Hanson and Henry (1992: 265): 'The challenge is to shape them into ongoing cycles of events where the separate parts reinforce the functioning of the whole.'

Questions Arising from the Study

- How does a primary school define its customers and other stake-holders?
- What is the link between effective marketing and school improvement?
- What is an appropriate balance of roles of staff, governors, local education authorities and consultants in school marketing?

Recommendations

- Schools actively build a shared recognition and understanding of marketing
- A senior member of staff is given designated responsibility for marketing
- A sub-committee of governors is established
- Marketing is clearly linked with other initiatives within school development planning
- Strategy becomes increasingly customer focused

References

Bagley, C., Woods, P. and Glatter, R. (1996) "Barriers to school responsiveness in the education quasi-market", *School Organisation*, 16, (1), 45-58.

Devlin, T. and Knight, B. (1990) *Public Relations and Marketing for Schools*. Harlow: Longman.

Gewirtz, S., Ball, S. and Bowe, R. (1995) *Markets, Choice and Equity in Education*. Milton Keynes: Open University Press.

Glover, D., Gough, G. and Johnson, M. (1996) "Home school links, *Managing Schools Today*, 6, (2), 37.

Gorard, S. (1999) "Well, that about wraps it up for school choice research: a state of the art review", *School Leadership and Management*, 19, (1), 25-47.

Hanson, E.M. and Henry, W. (1992) "Strategic marketing for educational systems", *School Organisation*, 12, (3), 255-67.

Harrison, M. and Gill, S. (1992) *Primary School Management*. Oxford: Heinemann.

Headington, R. and Howson, J. (1995) "The school brochure: a marketing tool?" *Education Management and Administration*, 23, (2), 89-95.

Keep, E. (1992) "Schools in the market place? Some problems with the private sector models", *British Journal of Education and Work*, 5, (2), 43-55.

Kotler, P. and Armstrong, G. (1996) *Principles of Marketing* (7th edn). London: Prentice Hall.

Kotler, P. and Andreasen, A.R. (1987) *Strategic Marketing for Non-profit Organisations* (3rd edn). London: Prentice Hall.

Smedley, D. (1995) "Marketing secondary schools to parents", *Education Management and Administration*, 23, (2), 96-103.

Warner, C. (1994) *Promoting Your School*. Thousand Oaks, California: Corwin Press Sage.

Woods, P. (1994) "School responses to the quasi-market" in M. Halstead, (ed.) *Parental Choice and Education*. London: Kogan Page.

Chapter Nine

Managing Failure

DURING an OFSTED inspection twelve months after being appointed as headteacher of a primary school Sue Merry was informed that it was quite likely that the school would be placed in special measures. In her words, 'at the time I was unsure of what that meant, the word "failure" being a more familiar term'. However, being an experienced headteacher, her response to the situation was to accept that decision and continue ways of improving the school standards in order that it could be removed from such a status. Not only did the achievement provide a good source of information in organisational terms but it subsequently provided her with the focus for a Master's dissertation, along with the credibility and the stature to research the experiences of other headteachers who found themselves in similar positions. As a 'fellow sufferer' she was able to construct and pilot such interview schedules as were acceptable to colleagues, in addition to visiting schools where many outsiders would be denied entry. Not withstanding that, there was still a price to pay as she outlined:

> Schools in special measures are already subjected to a great deal of stress and consideration will need to be given to this factor. I will need to be sensitive to the feelings of the headteachers who may have already undergone the process of inspection, will be undergoing close monitoring by HMI and LEA and facing another inspection before their removal from special measures.

The Study

Drawing on the individual key issues and action plan of each school, Merry sought to support a semi-structured interview schedule with documentary evidence gathered from ten primary schools across three local education authorities. Tape recordings allowed her more opportunity for reflection and analysis following the question piloting with a headteacher colleague whose school had recently been removed from the special measures category. Reflecting on her trial interview, Merry found that unsolicited information about the school's plight was proffered, rather than the personal biography of the interviewee that she had sought. Such a situation led to an amended schedule being produced (see Appendix 9.1).

The headteacher biographies, reflecting fairly traditional career routes to management, monopolised the space available. For this reason, the summary chart (see Figure 9.1) is intended to facilitate the process and thus provide scope for further comment.

Results and Analysis

Although the emphasis was on gaining factual information, the impression-istic nature of the process was revealed through a number of sub-questions which appeared to go off at a tangent rather than probe the initial responses. Given the sensitivity of the situation this is understandable, the question of changes in school organisation (see Appendix 9.1) would have been quite revealing in disclosing any commonality of response.

Pathway to Headship: Changes in School Organisation

Responses reflected a common dilemma for governors and the local educa-tion authority. Given the traditional pathways to headship few experienced headteachers will have had experience of managing special measures situations successfully. Often those who have will have been subjected to considerable stress as the researcher found out. Yet, whilst accepting the need to motivate staff and establish systems, is there a place for specific leadership training and team-building courses as the first point of support rather than relying on *ad hoc* consultancy and feedback from associate head-teachers and the local education authority? In short, an attempt to promote

School description	Catchment	Number on roll	H/T Status	Schools current position	Key issue for action	Staff teaching turnover	Parent's reaction	Validity as a basis for improvement
A – urban CP	Relatively poor	272	In post during inspection	Recently removed from special measures	Poor pupil attainment	No staff changes, some resistance to change, build on enthusiasm	Initial problems but gained support following meetings	Can see process does result in improvement
B – urban CP plus Nursery	Deprived area, 20% travelling families	303 + 53 p/t Nursery	Seconded after inspection subsequently appointed	Recently removed from special measures	Quality of teaching and learning	Many staff changes, much resistance, blame dumping, staff needed re-assurance	Immediate support	Staff would not agree that inspection facilitated school improvement – not worth the trauma
C – urban CP	Deprived area on the edge of two council estates	269	In post during inspection	Recently removed from special measures	Quality of teaching and learning	Many staff changes, some resistance, negativity	Immediate support	Inspection and special measures did not facilitate improvement

Figure 9.1:   Headteacher biographies

School	Pupils	Area/Intake	Appointment	Special measures	Issue	Staff changes	Governors	Inspection
D – Voluntary aided C of E	145	Urban priority area	Appointed after inspection	Still in special measures		Staff not surprised at decision, aware of problems, not subsequent changes, little resistance, weekend training courses	Initial problems but gained support following meetings	Agreed that inspection had facilitated improvement but later in the process – staff were confident now
E – Urban CP	157	High ethnic minority intake	Appointed just prior to inspection. Previous H/T moved to another headship	Just been placed in special measures	Reduction of budget deficit	Number of staff changes	Change of chair of governors but general lack of interest	Unable to comment
F – Voluntary aided C of E	390	High ethnic minority intake	Appointed after special measures but on long term sick leave associate head cover	Currently special measures but anticipating re-inspection	Poor pupil attainment	Many staff changes	General lack of interest	Staff would agree inspection facilitated improvement

Figure 9.1: Headteacher biographies

(continued over)

G – Suburban CP	Deprived area with high ethnic minority intake	402	Acting head for inspection now permanent	Currently special measures but re-inspection date fixed	Quality of teaching and learning Academic outcomes not really considered	Two changes (one voluntary) staff particularly upset, genuinely believed they were effective	General lack of interest	Yes, but trauma unacceptable Staff wary of making suggestions
H – Voluntary aided RC	Deprived area	110 + 48 p/t Nursery	In post during inspection	Recently removed from special measures	Quality of teaching and learning	Majority on sick leave, only school deemed to have satisfactory leadership	Immediate support loyal and acknow-ledge improve-ment that had been made	Unable to comment, but felt success fragile, staff turnover an issue
I – Voluntary aided C of E	Rural area with few social problems	61	Appointed after inspection	Recently removed from special measures	Poor pupil attainment	Complete staff turnover, H/T appeared worn down by process	Immediate support	
J – CP	Area of high un-employment	286 52 p/t Nursery	Appointed after inspection	Recently removed from special measures	Quality of teaching and learning Academic outcomes not really considered	Reduction of 3 staff achieved voluntarily	Lack of parental interest	Agreed inspection had facilitated improvement

Figure 9.1:   Headteacher biographies

a vision mapping of the future that seeks to provide realistic situations:

> Successful heads are *goal-orientated* insofar as they have vision of how they would like to see their school develop. Thus, they give the school a direction and are capable of operationalising their goals and values both through a long-term strategy and at the level of their day to day action. (Newton and Tarrant, 1992: 218-19; original italics)

However, these headteachers, unless newly appointed, have largely not been successful leaders or at least their performance has dipped at some stage. For as Sale (1997: 34) argued:

> A leader not concerned with strategic management would probably not be leading at all.

In the case of those appointed after inspection, the issue of theory and practice is just as relevant. Both Mortimore (1988) and Myers (1997) provided checklists for effectiveness, yet neither attempted to quantify the amount of 'purposeful' or 'professional' leadership necessary to tip the school into the effectiveness segment. Equally, how small could the involvement of teachers or lack of vision be to relegate it into the special measures category? Deming's (1986: 19) views on profound knowledge, particularly as they apply to education, merit consideration: 'Experience alone, without theory, teaches management nothing about what to do to improve … '

The Effects on Staff and Governors

This question focused on the impact of failure on staff and governors. As Figure 9.1 shows, for the former this was considerable with only School D teachers being aware of the extent of their problems. Staff in Schools G and J genuinely believed they were effective through the provision of a secure and happy environment for the pupils. Whilst it was easy to catalogue teaching turnover, information on governing bodies was less forthcoming due to the numbers of headteachers in post for the original inspection. What can be ascertained is that the chairs of governors in schools A, E and J all registered whilst schools C and G underwent considerable changes in membership. Furthermore, all the schools sampled benefited from two additional governors in response to OFSTED's recommendations.

Key Issues prior to Inspection: Measures to Address them

The headteacher in School A claimed to have been aware of all but two of the issues identified in the report, a situation shared by headteacher G. The headteachers of schools B, F and I had not been in post at the time of inspection, whilst the remainder confessed that they knew of the issues but had not managed to address them yet.

Staff Involvement

Responses to question four reflected discrepancies and apparent inconsistency in the process with two schools claiming that the inspection team ignored their development plans. For others the view that implementation was unfeasible or impractical based on evidence gathered from observation appears to be another explanation. As the headteacher of School A insisted: 'For the first time the school had a proper development plan. It was totally ignored by the inspection team.' Conversely, School E claimed that recognition of the school development plan and the contribution it would continue to make was given by the inspection team. Schools B, F and I could not provide any information, as the headteachers had not been in post at the time of the inspection (see Figure 9.1). Schools D and I had no development plans, and although the remaining eight schools all had plans, only schools A and G were implementing them.

Involvement with Action Plan

The question of involvement and ownership of the action plan was perhaps an example of the iceberg theory of school management, where what the researcher reported did not fully reveal the submerged tensions and inactivity. This has implications for future teamwork and collaborative working: a feature that headteacher A recognised in his comment 'collaborative working now in place'. It would have been fruitful to have investigated this area more fully, particularly the way headteachers appointed after the inspection used certain strategies to motivate staff and create an effective team.

Changes in Classroom Monitoring

Responses were seen to be more positive. As Merry stated:

The systems set up in all the schools provided for monitoring curriculum coverage and standards attained by the pupils in addition to classroom observations for monitoring the teaching and learning taking place. It was seen by staff and headteachers alike to have had a very positive effect within the school.

She went on to say that 'as none of the schools had monitoring systems in place prior to inspection it could be assumed that headteachers were not fully aware of what was going on in the classroom'. Here there seems to be an opportunity for further discussion and questioning of headteachers regardless of their school situations. Recent research across a sample of high achieving primary schools in the north west of England compared with others deemed to be performing less well, although by no means in special measures, revealed classroom monitoring systems to be at the core of higher achievement. As suggested (Smith and Sykes, 1999: 25) in a report to an local education authority, schools currently achieving higher than expected results, termed 'transforming schools':

> enjoy the leadership of heads who have a sound knowledge of the curriculum across key stages and are noticeable for their structures which enable them to maintain a high visibility and degree of both formal and informal monitoring.

However, the monitoring process extends further in such schools where curriculum co-ordinators accept monitoring and evaluating as part of their role, together with planning and delivery of in-service training. Thus the climate of the school is established, leading to increased professional development or empowerment as Marks and Louis (1997: 247) identified:

> We regard the empowerment of teachers as an essential condition for building an intellectually focused school culture – that is, a school culture focused on teaching and learning.

Inspection as Improvement, Teachers' Influence

The messages here provoked some sharp responses along with a realisation about the importance of their role. Comments like:

> 'they now see what they do affects what happens overall;'

'they can now see the link with progression and continuity;'

'everyone geared up to improve standards throughout;'

are particularly heartening, although there is also cause for concern that matters had progressed to such a poor state before being addressed. Clearly there can be no doubt as to the degree of managerial neglect as exemplified in the lack of self-evaluation, internal review or strategic planning and all respondents agreed, with reluctance and reservations about the process, that inspection facilitates school improvement:

> 'I don't like the process but I can see the outcome does result in school improvement.' (School A, headteacher)

> 'It has been instrumental in making tremendous change but it should not have been necessary. Advisers should have been aware.' (School C, headteacher)

> 'I would say yes we have improved but the trauma of special measures may be unacceptable.' (School G, headteacher)

Moreover, the headteacher of School G was emphatic that being appointed after the event provided him with a ready-made starting point to apply what Fidler 1997) described as 'contingent leadership':

> it is personal action which is at the core of leadership. On the other hand ... leadership should be contingent. What is appropriate leadership at a particular point in time depends on: the context and its prehistory; the nature of followers; the particular issues involved; in addition to the predispositions of the leader. Thus, although a leader may have a preferred leadership style, this may need to be varied according to circumstances.

Such comments are worth balancing against the views of total quality management advocates, most notably, Deming, whose views many forward-looking schools have adopted in their search for improvement. Despite his concerns about mass inspection, 'Inspection to improve quality is too late, ineffective, costly', Deming would have been concerned both about the lack of leadership training and the ignorance about processes for improvement.

Staff Development Procedures

On the question of staff development, Deming (1986) emphasised the importance of creating an environment which encouraged education within an organisation:

> Institute a vigorous programme of education, and encourage self-improvement for everyone. What an organisation needs is not just good people; it needs people that are improving with education. Advances in competitive position will have their roots in knowledge. (quoted in Neave, 1990: 47)

Analysing Merry's research in this area, responses to her questions about staff development procedures are particularly revealing. If prior to inspection, five out of the ten schools sampled had no systems or procedures in place, how did they account for school standards funds monies? What was the role of the local education authority in auditing expenditure? As Merry revealed, a collaborative approach had now been employed based on the action plan, noting that 'they [schools] were making use of talents and encouraging staff to take responsibility for their own development', surely a minimum professional requirement today highlighted by Kanter (1990: 324) ten years previously:

> Hereinafter the employee will assume full responsibility for his own career – for keeping his qualifications up to date, for getting himself moved to the next position at the right time, for salting away funds for retirement, and, most daunting of all, for achieving job satisfaction. The company, while making no promises, will endeavour to provide a conducive environment, economic exigencies permitting.

For others, staff development was inextricably linked to motivation and provides an essential ingredient in effective leadership:

> Leaders must engage followers such that there is mutual commitment to the shared purpose of building the best of organisations. Followers, it is claimed, can be motivated to give more of themselves. (Angus, 1989: 69)

Resistance to Changes post-OFSTED: Staff Motivation

The issue of staff resistance was well catalogued by Merry and is summarised in Figure 9.1. Her interpretation of the varying motivational forces is revealing, with many headteachers seeing their first task as restoring professional self-esteem for what some considered almost a professional bereavement as in the case of School B. For schools D, G and J, all the teachers appeared relieved to have the necessary changes implemented for them in order to attain the ultimate goal: removal from special measures. Once again Angus's views on reward are applicable:

> In return for effort, productivity, loyalty and so on, leaders offer rewards of one kind or another to subordinates. These may be tangible payments, promotion or improved conditions, or may be in the form of less obvious but especially important matching of respective needs so that both leaders and followers get some satisfaction (or at least reduction of antagonism) out of the exchange. (69)

Support from the Local Education Authority

Questions of support evoked some illuminating responses that cast a shadow on local authority practice and efficiency. Comments reflected what Merry termed the 'steep learning curve' experienced by many local education authority personnel. However, this does not excuse the unfortunate experiences of School A where the adviser was changed three times along with a request by the headteacher to remove the associate headteacher as she considered him inappropriate to her needs. Likewise, parental support varied as Figure 9.1 shows. Not unnaturally, the greatest consistency was found to come from HMI who reportedly 'gave clear focused feedback and established good relationships with heads and staff' resulting in mutual respect and raised morale. Such comments led to comparisons with the original OFSTED teams who compared much less favourably. In a detailed conclusion two strands of headteacher under-performance were identified as discussed. First is the question of monitoring. As Merry recorded

> None of the schools had had any formalised systems in place for monitoring prior to inspection. It is perhaps one of the simplest and most effective ways of determining the overall effectiveness of a school.

It is worthwhile exploring the reasons for this in more detail. Clearly due to the sensitive nature of the research, explanations are not readily available from the interview data. Nevertheless, other commissioned research carried out for a local education authority (Smith and Sykes, 1999), highlighted the fact that by no means was it a situation confined to the worst performing schools. One of the key differences in the more detailed survey, over a range of high-achieving and under-performing schools, lay in the degree of monitoring that took place and the status accorded it by the head-teacher. Fidler and Atton (1999: 93) distinguished between the two aspects of headship; the leading professional and the chief executive. For the former, teaching and educational vision was seen to be dominant whilst management, relationships and leadership comprised the executive role. It would be easy simply to identify the problems of special measures schools through a breakdown of one area of headteacher performance. However, failure to manage systems and procedures, together with a commitment to-wards continuous improvement, is clearly apparent. To what extent this can be traced to a misplaced educational philosophy that respects and up-holds the teacher's professionalism and creativity, yet rejects any notion of stand-ardisation of competency factors as outlined by the Teacher Training Agency, is questionable. Certainly Ribbins (1999) railed against the pres-criptive training programme which reduced school leadership to a manager-ial enterprise and tick list. For these schools a more standardised work pattern might have ensured that staff stayed on track.

Future of the School

The final area of questioning focused on the vision and the future of the school. Not surprisingly all wished to see removal from special measures and build on achievements, with one respondent citing the possibility of excel-lence in ICT and another stressing recognition as an excellent community school as their goal. For others an element of self-doubt was detectable often due to the strain of the re-inspection process and constant need to lift morale. Interestingly only one headteacher referred to the fragile nature of the school's status in the light of recruitment, a factor that impacts particul-arly in more disadvantaged areas. Further comment on the processes of empowering teachers would have been useful at this point. This together with a more shared approach to management that Hargreaves and Hopkins (1991) argued would help embed the changes and impacts on the success already achieved.

Reflections on the Study

A number of issues arise here in a chapter that highlights under-performance by professionals at all levels. First is the disproportionate number of schools in special measures which serve areas of considerable disadvantage. Ouston's (1999) paper drew attention to this discrepancy and, whilst in no way excusing under-performance, there would appear to be a need for increased resources if long-term standards were to be maintained.

Second is the question of the retention and development of staff. All the schools surveyed appeared deficient in staff development and collaborative working. Whilst the latter is difficult to assess without detailed knowledge, the question of staff development opportunities could begin to be recorded on request by local education authorities and even electronically as part of regular monitoring operation. Through the use of simple data collection authorities would receive an annual record of every teachers' participation in professional development programmes outside the five statutory days. Whilst some might blanch at a further bureaucratic request, when linked to school standards funds monies, this would at least ensure that a picture of participating schools, and by implication absentee schools, would begin to emerge. Hence these schools that fell below a certain take-up rate of in-service activity might be the focus of greater attention by advisers in their pastoral role. For those who view such a policy as further evidence of local authority interference it is pertinent to perhaps remind people of the enormous burden placed on local education authorities when a schools is deemed to be in special measures. Ultimately, any process that can effectively target resources and improve performance must be welcome.

The third issue is concerned with the timing of inspections. Evidence from this study suggests that the local education authority gathers insufficient performance data after the resignation of a headteacher. The request for a light touch inspection and detailed action plan by the deputy headteacher and local education adviser would help pave the way for a new incumbent. Finally, it is worth reflecting on the new performance threshold and to what extent it will be effective in helping eliminate under-performance. One approach would be to make it a statutory requirement for all co-ordinators holding more than one responsibility point to undertake statutory training in strategic planning, target setting, team building and leadership every five years as part of their continuing professional development portfolio.

Merry's research carried out with an early cohort of failing schools in this sense is probably unique. Recent reports from OFSTED (1998) recognise the improvements that all schools have made particularly in key stage test scores. Although the move is now towards identifying the more complacent advantaged schools, it would nevertheless appear unlikely that such a large number of primary schools would ever fall into the special measures category again.

Recommendations

- A local education authority adviser/inspector to maintain closer contact with schools at risk and conduct pre-inspection checks
- Advisory teachers/consultants to provide in-service programmes termly
- A database of curriculum co-ordinators holding two + responsibility points, to be established in every local education authority as a means to encourage professional up-dating
- Deputies seeking a headship to be offered a one term secondment as associate heads (to be funded out of school standards monies, or part of an exchange scheme)
- Governors of Beacon schools to be co-opted to schools at risk

Appendix 9.1

Interview Questions

(1) (a) Can you briefly describe your pathway to headship?

(b) What changes in school organisation have you implemented here?

(2) (a) What was the effect of the school being placed in special measures on the staff and the governors?

(b) Have there been any changes in the staffing?

(c) Have there been any changes in the governing board?

(3) (a) Of the key issues identified which were you already aware of prior to inspection?

    (b)   What measures had been taken to address them?

(4) (a)   Was there a working school development plan in place prior to inspection?

    (b)   Who had been involved in its production and implementation?

    (c)   And how?

(5) (a)   Who was involved in writing the action plan?

    (b)   And how?

(6) (a)   What systems were in place for classroom monitoring?

    (b)   Have there been any changes?

    (c)   When, what and how?

(7) (a)   To what extent do your classroom teachers feel their practice influences the effectiveness of the school?

    (b)   Do they view inspection as facilitating school improvement?

    (c)   Do you?

(8) (a)   What procedures and systems were in place for staff development?

    (b)   Have there been any changes?

    (c)   Can you outline them?

(9) (a)   Have you encountered any resistance to the changes brought about post OFSTED?

    (b)   What form did it take?

    (c)   How did you motivate staff to overcome it?

(10) (a)   Can you give me an outline of the support you and your school have received from the LEA since being placed in special measures?

    (b)   The governors?

    (c)   The parents?

    (d)   HMI?

(11) What do you see as the future for you and your school?

(12) Is there anything you wish to add?

References

Angus, L. (1989) "New leadership and the possibility of educational reform" in J. Smyth (ed.) *Critical Perspectives on Educational Leadership*. (Reprinted 1998) London: Falmer Press.

Deming, W.E. (1986) *Out of the Crisis: Quality, Productivity and Competitive Position*. Cambridge: Cambridge University Press.

Fidler, B. (1997) "School leadership: some key ideas", *School Leadership and Management*, 17, (1), 23-37.

Fidler, B. and Atton, T. (1999) *Poorly Performing Staff in Schools and How to Manage Them: Compatibility, Competence and Motivation*. London: Routledge.

Hargreaves, D.H. and Hopkins, D. (1992) *The Empowered School*. London: Cassell.

Kanter, R.M. (1990) *The Change Masters*. London: Unwin.

Marks, H.M. and Louis, K.S. (1997) "Does teacher empowerment affect the classroom? The implications of teacher empowerment for instructional practice and student academic performance", *Educational Evaluation and Policy Analysis*, 19, (3), 245-75.

Mortimore, P. (1988) *The Junior School Project*. London: ILEA.

Myers, K. (1997) *The Intelligent School*. London: Paul Chapman.

OFSTED (1998) *Making Headway*. London: OFSTED Publications.

Ouston, J. (1999) "Education, policy and equity in the inner cities". Paper presented at BEMAS Conference, Manchester: UMIST.

Neave, H.R. (1990) *The Deming Dimension*. Knoxville USA: SPC Press.

Newton, C. and Tarrant, T. (1992) *Managing Change in Schools*. London: Routledge.

Ribbins, P. (1999) "Educational administration and the search for Sophia". Paper presented at BEMAS Conference, Manchester: UMIST.

Sale, J. (1997) "Performance is personal", *Managing Schools Today*, 7, (2), 34-6.

Smith, A. and Sykes, C. (2000) "The soft fruits of school improvement". Paper presented at BERA Conference, Cardiff: University of Cardiff.

Chapter Ten

Conclusion

TAKEN together these chapters can be seen to present a snapshot of primary school management, to borrow from Boyes' title. As a snapshot it is reminiscent of the traditional, whole school photograph, representing as it does, the views and experiences of dozens of teachers, interpreted through the lenses of the eight teacher researchers and finally cropped and framed by the authors. Like any photographic record, the collection provides a unique moment of social history.

Looking back through an album it is not always the subject matter in the foreground that engages our attention, but often the details of a familiar landscape or room that has been subtly, or radically, altered in the intervening years. The pace of change in education is well documented throughout each chapter and, in some cases, only months after a piece of research was completed, actual and qualitative changes can be recorded. (For example, some research was carried out in schools designated as grant maintained, a designation that has ceased to exist. Another instance was indicated in Chapter 9. Schools were less likely on average, at the time of writing this book, to be placed in special measures following an OFSTED inspection.) It is possible to identify emerging themes that form a shared background to chapters, which focus on various aspects of primary school management.

By identifying these themes, the authors intend in this concluding chapter, not only to explore some of the underlying concerns of primary practitioners at the beginning of the twenty-first century, but also to examine the nature of some of the recommendations made by both the researchers and the authors in the light of this broader, developing picture of primary school management. For this snapshot is not a static social document but one which attempts to portray what *is*, with inevitable, inherent limitations as well as one which suggests approaches to an improved future for our schools.

Each of the eight studies was conducted within the north west of England, an area as diverse as any in the United Kingdom. Neither the researchers nor the authors would claim that the samples or data on which the reflections are based were representative of a wider national picture. The issues raised, however, are likely to be of relevance and interest to those involved in primary school management in any context.

Change has always been the overarching concern of all the writers. Throughout the teachers' responses there was evidence of a profession that accepted change as the norm and was eager to embrace reform that concurred with their beliefs about best practice, an optimism apparent in the answers of deputy headteachers interviewed by Goggin. In a number of chapters there was significant support expressed in favour of the national literacy and numeracy strategies, for example, to illustrate answers to more general questions. Although there was perhaps a lingering bewilderment in some schools about expectations and how to achieve progress, nowhere was there a suggestion that schools or teachers were trying to evade or sabotage school improvement initiatives.

Observations of how schools were faring in their attempts to balance imposed change and change initiated at school level, permeate most of the chapters. Boyes' research found that schools were unable to exercise their own management capability for decision-making in relation to their local circumstances and, possibly more worryingly, teachers unable to use professional judgement in the classroom. A surprising number of current MA students are researching teacher stress. An impression from scanning the raw data was that teachers, far from making ritual complaints about workload, were able to identify specific factors causing stress that include reference to the balance between their autonomy and external pressures. In this book, the role of OFSTED and the effects of standard assessment tests and league tables featured in many responses. Both Bennett and Boyes made recommendations about school self-evaluation as a tool for school improvement, with Boyes looking for a reduction in the 'noise' created by annually published results, recommending the triennial submission of results to OFSTED for monitoring purposes. Schools seemed impatient to be allowed to control their own destinies, armed now with expertise gained, sometimes painfully, from inspections, national initiatives and testing, yet seemingly adolescents struggling towards full maturity, as the chapters document weaknesses in strategic aspects of management. Nevertheless, unless the apron strings are at least loosened, the opportunity for schools to become centres for sustainable improvement may be missed.

Two major assumptions about the management of change and primary school management can be traced across the different researchers' work. First they focused on the need for skilled human resource management to ensure successful school improvement and second, they identified school development planning as the key mechanism for initiating, implementing and tracking innovation.

There is much to celebrate in teachers' answers which indicated a perception that they were each making a contribution to whole school development. A shared understanding of purpose was expressed, particularly in response to questions from Bennett, Boyes and Parkinson.

Difficult to define, although its power was felt throughout, is a notion of professionalism. This professionalism was rooted, as Boyes believed, in a commitment to provide the best education for children. In the face of change, values have to be re-examined and the question addressed by each school and teacher; what is now the best education for children? Misunderstandings about the role marketing might play in school development and a level of resistance to new technologies provide evidence of this process, in the research conducted by Core and Singleton. It is however a process in which teachers want to have their professional voice heard. As articulated by respondents, this professionalism brought a curious vulnerability. At a time when teachers have grown to appreciate the benefits of working together to manage change, conscientious staff seem hampered in their efforts to develop effective teamwork and plan strategically by the need to keep up with demands in their own classrooms. The pressure of teacher workload was never far from the surface in these surveys. Parkinson found headteachers unsure about the appropriate balance of responsibility between themselves and their staff; Goggin identified a lack of clarity in expectations of deputy headship and there was widespread concern about the lack of an effective role for curriculum co-ordinators. A fear remained, despite awareness and belief in the cycle of planning, monitoring, evaluation and review, that time given to it might be a distraction from the central purpose. Merry's research in schools that were not successful should have the power to dispel such doubts. Weaknesses in planning and collaborative working in her sample lay at the heart of their under-achievement.

Most primary schools were typified by co-operative adult relationships and by open communication. Harmonious relationships are vital in any successful organisation and according to Bennett larger organisations have something to learn from primary schools. School leaders are faced with the challenge of harnessing this strength and transforming it into effective teamwork. Parkinson's research showed that the necessary understanding of how to do this was patchy amongst headteachers. Where they have a vision for the school it is not always translated into management decisions that developed staff in their roles to accomplish stated goals. Goggin's research into the role of the deputy headteacher underlined how important the headteacher's management style was in determining the effectiveness and level of involvement of other members of staff. Teachers' involvement in whole school development, where it did occur, was reported by Parkinson, Braddock, Goggin and others to be operational rather than strategic. Boyes tended to view this as acceptable, demonstrating well understood responsibilities. There was, without doubt, some acceptance of unextended roles within the samples. Goggin noted this amongst deputy headteachers. Singleton found that ICT curriculum co-ordinators, although a special case in some respects, were hindered by not having more of a direct strategic role. Most of the researchers called for better-defined roles and responsibilities.

The reasons for this lack of clarity may originate, as suggested above in a relatively unevolved professionalism and a response to the pace of change that cried, 'too little time'. In addition, the researchers explored at all staff levels, the depth of understanding about a collaborative approach to school improvement and strategic planning. They generally found awareness but in many cases limited knowledge. Once again Merry's research indicated that cohesion is not a desirable luxury but a prerequisite for effectiveness, a conclusion supported by Parkinson's data and reflections. Merry, Bennett, Goggin, Boyes and Core all recommended professional development, specifically to address this area of weakness.

Teachers in many of the samples expressed positive views about continuing professional development. The management of continuing professional development was an area of satisfaction for staff in Parkinson's research and Boyes' respondents identified extended professional development as a right. Management education and training had not been undertaken by all senior managers in the samples, whilst curriculum co-ordinators were unlikely to have attended anything other than subject-based courses. Efforts to link training programmes with national standards as undertaken in 1998 might well pay dividends in shared understanding of management issues in the future.

Teaching staff may have learned to co-operate and co-ordinate some aspects of their work. The researchers discovered that other stakeholders in education were kept on the margins and their involvement in school development was minimal. In some cases observations on the roles of adults other than teachers were not central to the research and so were not fully analysed. Bennett and Parkinson both commented on the lack of formal communication with classroom assistants. The expansion in both numbers and range of responsibilities for non-teaching members of staff at the time of writing had yet to be adequately addressed in management terms. Braddock's findings in relation to the limited part some governors played in development planning were alarming given the responsibilities placed upon them. She was also able to present positive examples. Where schools had built effective partnerships they could be encouraged to share that expertise. Merry suggested that governors from Beacon schools could be co-opted to advise schools in difficulties, and Core proposed that governors should be involved more systematically in promoting and in marketing schools. Parents were even less likely to have an influence on policy-making. Braddock found the same cool attitude in schools to parental surveys as Core, who believed schools must become more customer-focused in order to improve. Parkinson proposed regular reviews of communication channels by a group of staff and other stakeholders.

The studies revealed something of the uncertain partnership between schools and local education authorities. Schools look to them as legitimate sources of advice and support at a time when local education authorities themselves are under scrutiny and pressure from government. Singleton showed the importance of local education involvement in implementing national policy with respect to ICT, in training and monitoring progress. Capacity to achieve this appears to be inadequate. An authority has a responsibility to identify and monitor under-performing schools. Some of Merry's respondents were critical of the level and quality of support they received. It is perhaps inevitable that schools in difficulty should seek to spread the blame. However, the fact that at the time of writing, fewer schools fail inspections may indicate that local education authorities have become better prepared to make helpful interventions. It was in Core's study of marketing that more fundamental questions about the relationship between an authority and its schools surfaced. Schools are left to promote themselves, yet the local education authority may recommend closure. If schools are ready to become self-sufficient, problem-solving organisations, what role is required of local education authorities? Should they merely provide a range of consultancy services or retain regulatory powers? The studies did not confront these issues, but in the background the debate is significant.

It is perhaps unsurprising that the researchers found weaknesses in school development planning and strategic planning where management of teamworking and partnerships are weak; where teachers are content to be consulted at a fairly superficial level or even simply informed, provided that it is done efficiently and courteously and where headteachers are unwilling or uncertain how much to delegate, even to their deputies.

Researching innovation and development (Bennett, Singleton and Core) and leadership (Boyes, Parkinson and Goggin), inevitably leads to questions and reflection on planning. These researchers gave ample evidence that it is taken seriously in primary schools and is, at the very least, intentionally a collaborative process. Braddock addressed the issue directly and Merry's research charted how some schools, unaccustomed to development planning, have taken on the challenge in response to OFSTED.

Braddock was able to quote the OFSTED finding that school development plans had improved. There is evidence across the chapters that they have become more sophisticated documents than the lengthy, wish-list of improvements that were not an uncommon first attempt in schools. What appears to be missing in some cases is a robust process to support them; a process featuring not just appropriate stakeholder participation in their preparation but also in the monitoring, evaluating and reviewing of progress towards the targets. Without this it is impossible for school leaders to give development plans priority in an informed manner.

Carefully directed management education for all school leaders might have lessened the need for Braddock to explain the difference between school development planning and strategic planning to render it possible for her question to be answered. It is worth reiterating that she viewed strategic planning as,

> focusing on the aims of education to bring together all the aspects of school's planning and thereby turn long term vision into short term goals to give teachers more control of the nature and pace of change.

If the school development plan has moved from the merely aspirational, in some places it is in danger of remaining a document of bureaucratic compliance. Braddock underlined the importance of drawing on it to determine practical initiatives to promote improvement in teaching and learning.

An under-developed capacity to use data to give priority to decision-making is a feature of the management of some schools in the samples. Boyes's respondents were generally not surprised by the key issues identified through the inspection process, suggesting that school self-evaluation had reached the point at which it could reliably identify weaknesses. In contrast Merry found some schools in her sample that were shaken to find that what amounted to little more than a 'gut feeling' of effectiveness was challenged by OFSTED judgements. In both surveys there was evidence that the inspection process had been instrumental in prompting schools to ask hard questions. Boyes and Bennett found that even where weaknesses were identified at school level there was less confidence in proposing remedies. Goggin suggested that schools are not good at establishing specific success criteria.

Core's, Boyes' and others' research contained examples of resistance to undesired effects of standard assessment tests and league tables. However, few teachers articulate clearly the ways in which numerical data is analysed and incorporated into a problem-solving approach to development planning and strategic plans for school improvement. Braddock believed that by not engaging in such careful analysis, schools left themselves open to external forces. One of Goggin's respondents suggested that the strength of development planning was to enable schools to personalise change. Currently it may be more realistic to scan the environment, gather and analyse data and subsequently to use development planning as a means of personalising change, that is likely to be dictated in pace and content, than to aim to control it. Flexible, informed, collaborative planning can prepare and educate all those involved with a school about improvement initiatives. Some respondents believed building a learning culture to be important in improving planning.

Where headteachers had focused on test scores and league tables as a lever for improvement it was open to misinterpretation by staff. Parkinson gave an example of one headteacher's attempt to encourage belief in the children's capacity to achieve higher standards that was perceived by staff as added pressure to pursue narrow classroom targets. This illustrates his findings that whilst strategic management appeared to be a strength in his sample, communication of the vision was relatively weak.

If teachers make scant and often vague references to provided sources of data such as PANDAS and results of national testing, no clearer picture is given of schools' own collection and employment of information. Bennett found little evidence of decision-making based on monitoring by curriculum co-ordinators. The bleakest picture was provided by Merry. Although only two schools in her sample were without school development plans prior to

OFSTED, not one had a formalised system for monitoring effectiveness. As part of post-OFSTED action plans monitoring had been introduced which staff believed had led to improvement.

Primary schools are portrayed as places where teaching staff work together with shared values, open communication and a belief in the importance of continuing professional development. There is a growing understanding of the way planning can be improved. A management structure exists of headteachers, deputy headteachers and curriculum co-ordinators, within a wider context that includes governors, parents and the local education authority. There is one finding common to many of the chapters that helps to answer why schools have not generally been as successful as they would wish at securing school improvement. There is little non-contact time for co-ordinators and deputy headteachers in many primary schools.

This appears to be a significant factor. For curriculum co-ordinators the opportunity to co-ordinate curriculum planning and monitor subject teaching and standards in the classroom becomes impossible, or so fragmented that it becomes difficult to argue for its effectiveness as a strategy. Co-ordinators in some cases reported a limited role, monitoring children's written work or tentatively advising other staff. Even deputy headteachers, who often carry a major responsibility for the curriculum, were found by Goggin to monitor teaching and learning irregularly, nor did they, as a rule, sit down and plan with the headteacher as a team.

This lack of opportunity may be to blame for the researchers' discovery of weaknesses in data handling and establishing success criteria by which to judge school effectiveness. Trial and error would allow schools to develop shared expertise in gathering and using information in a systematic way. Non-contact time could also enable teachers to undertake management training. It is worth noting again that the schools with poor inspection results were required to put in formal systems of monitoring, evaluation and review and now enjoyed the fruits of this approach. In Goggin's sample the deputy headteachers who had established successful monitoring systems had engaged in study for the national professional qualification for headship.

We are, of course, aware that provision of non-contact time in schools is complex and schools operate within many constraints, not least financial ones. However, it is hard to see how curriculum co-ordinators can meet the national standards laid down by the Teacher Training Agency (1998) for subject leaders or schools meet the growing demands, from inside and without, for self-evaluation and school improvement, if the issue is not addressed at school and national policy levels.

Some areas of resistance had surfaced to ways of working that would prompt a greater monitoring role for middle and senior managers, necessitating increased non-contact time. Parkinson, in particular, found headteachers hesitant to delegate responsibility. This was, he suggested, as a result of uncertainty about appropriate levels of responsibility and possibly a concern not to dilute their vision for the school. Even though respondents felt the inspection process had brought improvements, teachers in Boyes' and Merry's samples referred to the trauma for staff. Co-ordinators and senior managers are aware of staff sensitivities about observation and this may be enough to keep staff out of each other's classrooms, feeling unable to communicate a supportive rather than judgmental role throughout the school. Bennett quoted the DfEE, DTI (1997) report that considered well-managed organisations to be, 'supportive yet stretching' and 'accountable yet blame free'. Most schools in the samples could not confidently claim an established culture to match these conditions, which could have profound implications for the implementation of performance management in schools where classroom observation by team leaders is to be linked with appraisal.

Teachers have expressed the view that performance-related pay will destroy teamwork. The researchers questioned the quality of team working. Parkinson found 'participative decision-making' a relatively weak management area and Bennett identified 'shared effort' as the lowest scoring category in her research. What may be under threat is the belief that effective team working is an ideal that can bring improvement, voluntarily engaged in by professionals and that, although there are organisational management structures for operational purposes, there is openness and equality between teachers. The majority of teachers in Boyes' research were in favour of teachers being rewarded according to the amount of work put in, rather than for being a 'star performer'.

Only Boyes' researched directly teachers' attitudes to raising standards. He revealed that teachers are still wary of standard assessment tests and their results, many believing that the curriculum emphasis becomes distorted, (Singleton's study referred to the difficulty of promoting ICT as a non-core subject), and also referred to the fact that simple comparison of results is a poor way to judge schools' effectiveness. If some teachers reject results of year-on-year national testing as a sufficient measure of quality, then it becomes a management priority to develop school-based success criteria and target-setting for teaching and learning. It is unwise to draw conclusions from what is not said, in answer to questions unasked. However, responses that explicitly mentioned raising standards appear conspicuous by their absence. 'School improvement' was asked and spoken about as a rather general term and rarely linked to comments about pupil achievement or standards of teaching and learning. That is not to say that the researchers and their respondents were not concerned with improving teaching and pupil achievement, Braddock, for one, believed that individual schools make a difference, but that there may be a professional reticence about aspects of work that could identify the 'star performer'. Core suggested, in relation to marketing, that teachers were willing to acknowledge that there was a market in operation but might simultaneously hold a belief that they were unable to influence it. Similarly teachers might subscribe to school improvement initiatives without being confident that they will gain control over outcomes.

Once again restricted participation in all stages of planning, implementation, monitoring, evaluation and review may have inhibited such confidence. Equally, as Boyes' suggested, it may also be a fear of the consequences of failure. Systematic experimentation where mistakes are viewed as part of the shared learning process would develop a profession, that in time could predict more accurately how specific improvements could be made in instruction and pupil learning.

To return to the analogy of the photograph, we could be accused in this conclusion of spending too much time squinting at the negative, instead of appreciating the full-colour print. All the studies found schools engaged in improvement activities and teachers who were open to change and positive about continuing professional learning. Finally, we would like to review some of the recommendations to form an idea of what the researchers would like to see in the picture in the future.

Headteachers and deputies would have training in human resource management, with a focus on empowerment of staff (Bennett and Goggin). This would allow for the examination of roles, responsibilities and expectations in relation to decision-making (Parkinson, Boyes, Bennett and Braddock) for all school leaders. The status of deputy headteachers would be considered and increased by adoption of the title, assistant headteacher (Goggin), allowing for better teamwork at senior manager level. Where possible there would be rotation of responsibilities with the headteacher (Goggin), and secondment of deputies as associate headteachers (Merry) for professional development. A minimum of two days non-contact time would be provided for management training and curriculum monitoring (Goggin). Other staff would have access to management training and so would be prepared to take a more collaborative role in change management (Bennett).

Local education authorities should keep a record of curriculum co-ordinators to encourage professional updating (Merry). There would be improved communication and increased involvement in planning by a range of stakeholders (Parkinson, Braddock and Core). Schools would clarify their relationships with local education authorities and other sources of assistance (Singleton, Merry and Core).

It seems probable that progress towards some of these recommendations will continue to be made by schools. The teacher researchers chose to investigate these overlapping, areas of management, leading them to make recommendations that reveal a large measure of commonality. Their choices, and the often informed and concerned responses, indicate that developing people to fulfil more influential roles, (both teachers and non-teachers), is recognised as a priority. Despite expressed anxieties, it is possible that performance management may aid this process, if it delivers real opportunities for professional development, including management training.

The value of such studies by working teachers cannot be under-estimated. For the individual researcher a source of expertise is built that can directly influence the development of a school. Challenging questions posed to colleagues can, and from the evidence in some of the chapters does, cause other teachers to think about familiar problems in new ways. For anyone working inside or outside the classroom and school, teacher research provides a rich and illuminating picture of current practice, frustrations and hopes for the future.

References

DfEE, DTI (1997) *Competitiveness through Partnerships with People*. London: Department of Trade and Industry's Innovation Unit.

Teacher Training Agency (TTA) (1998) *National Standards for Subject Leaders*. London: TTA.

Index